Raging Grace

& other ramblings from the chaotic mind of Dave Hopwood

Also by Dave Hopwood:

Top Stories – 31 parables retold with contemporary comments

Pulp Gospel – 31 bits of the Bible retold with comments

Breaking into the Good Book – A novel for adults of all ages about three folk who break into the biblical stories via a clutch of wires and some green, smoking liquid

Film & Faith – Movie clips that bring the Bible to life

Diary of a Wimpy Christian – In which Dave does his best to boast about his weaknesses in an honest, humorous kind of way

Useful Stuff – Readings and dialogues for getting the Bible off the page

Spondulix – A tale of crime, greed, guns and cash and what happens when you put them all together

The Shed – A novel. 40 days in a shed with a disgruntled guy, and the pilgrims, stragglers and wanderers he encounters

For more info have a look at Dave's website –

davehopwood.com

For Simeon Wood.
Thank you for so much
encouragement,
laughter
& inspiration.
'A-ha!'

Raging Grace

& other ramblings from the chaotic mind of Dave Hopwood

Originally published on Dave's website:
davehopwood.com

Raging Grace

My very good friend and all-round top musician/dad/person/entertainer Simeon Wood sometimes does seminars about music styles and the Christian faith. During this he plays a series of versions of the classic hymn *Amazing Grace.* The one he plays by The Dropkick Murphys is my favourite. (You can find this on YouTube if you look for it.) It's fast, loud and played to a raucous crowd in a beery hall.

Now I'm well aware that this punk version of *Amazing Grace* by The Dropkick Murphys may not be to everyone's taste, (you may well have never heard it) and some may even find it totally unacceptable. But being an ageing punk fan I was immediately grabbed by the energy of the rendition, and watching it now on YouTube a shedload of thoughts come to me. Who would have thought a room full of folks at a gig like this would have been found singing John Newton's classic song of salvation? And for the entire world to watch on YouTube?

Amazing Grace was first published in 1779, 230-plus years ago, and John Newton wrote it following his own conversion and life transformation. Caught in a storm at sea, he cried out to God for help. John had been a slave trader and certainly knew what life was about. He'd rubbed shoulders with the people who moved in the most squalid circles. Some for the money, many because they were prisoners in chains. I wondered what he would have made of this – his gospel classic being pumped out of amps across that sweaty, beery hall.

My guess is he might be well-pleased. Surely he'd want this amazing, raging grace to be resounding in places just like this. I noticed that beneath the clips on YouTube of both live and studio versions of this song, there are comments about folks wanting this track played at their funeral. Now, I reckon

Amazing Grace sung at a punk gig is not that different to Jesus taking the stories and acts of God onto the sweaty, murky streets of Galilee and Jerusalem, amongst the open sewers, rife poverty and seething cries for revolution.

To race for a moment to the other end of the musical spectrum, in 1999 Cliff Richard took *The Millennium Prayer* to number one in the Radio 1 charts. It stayed in the charts for four months and was at number one for three weeks. Some radio stations refused to play it, yet it became the best-selling single of 1999 and the third biggest-selling single of Cliff's career. Some of us obviously did like it. Over the years it has been much-maligned but I can't help thinking that Cliff was doing a great thing, just like The Dropkick Murphys, bringing a prayer of hope to a new generation. The church put out its own millennium prayer around that time, but I think it's been largely forgotten.

Cliff sometimes gets a lot of stick, both for his style and his faith, but I will always remember wandering into a chip shop in High Wycombe, sometime around Christmas 1991, and hearing a little family happily singing his chart-topping *Saviour's Day*. Songs stay with us. I'm sure John Newton never imagined for one moment that there'd be a punk version of his song. But I'm glad there is.

Even Jesus Needed Other People

Just been reading about the time Jesus got baptised in Nick Page's excellent book *The Wrong Messiah*. His thoughts about why Jesus got baptised set me thinking.

Before John the Baptist came along (one of the few people in the world with 'the' as a middle name by the way, along with Attila the Hun, Elizabeth the First and Rupert the Bear) water baptism was a ritual gentiles undertook when they wanted to convert to Judaism. It was a sign of leaving behind the old life and beginning a new one. John is using it as a sign for leaving behind sin and beginning again. The remarkable thing was this – he invited Jews to do it too. Everyone was called by John to leave behind the old and start the new. That said, why did Jesus get baptised? Surely he didn't need to repent of any sin or leave behind an old life?

Well, for a clue it's worth looking back to Mary's cousin Elizabeth, a few shepherds at the manger and an elderly couple in the temple in Jerusalem. For a while Mary is the only one in the world who knows she is carrying the son of God, or even that she is pregnant at all. She must have had days when she wondered if it had all been a dream, if she had imagined the angel. If she was really carrying a baby at all. And then she sees her cousin Elizabeth. And what happens? Without any prompting at all her cousin announces to her that not only is she pregnant, but she is carrying God's child. She confirms to Mary that this is not a dream, this is real. This remarkable story is really happening. That must have meant so much to the young and frightened girl from Nazareth.

Cut to the manger and a few grunting shepherds elbowing their way into the Christmas scene. Joe must have wondered why on earth these dodgy social outcasts had blundered into the picture. Thank goodness they were a long way from home and the neighbours couldn't see who they were mixing with. Then the shepherds start yakking about angels and signs in the sky and suddenly everything changes. Suddenly strangers are confirming to this lowly, insecure couple that they have not imagined this story. Nine months down the line it is all coming true, Mary really is the mother of God's baby, Joe really is the adoptive father. The outcast shepherds have no other reason in the world to invade their space, unless they really have just seen messengers from God who have told them to come and confirm the story.

And the shepherds of course love this manger stuff – God in a trough? Brilliant! If he'd been in a palace they'd have had no chance of getting near, here in the muck and the straw they can actually touch those tiny fingers, smell that new baby smell (!) and tickle the child's cheek! Plus no one else has bothered to show up so they have this miracle baby all to themselves, thanks very much. And later, when they finally leave, they won't shut up, they're telling everyone else in Bethlehem. Bethlehem has welcomed a king tonight and they didn't even know it. Not till those shepherds banged on a few doors. Sadly of course, Bethlehem would pay the price too. Herod's men would see to that – the first group of people to be persecuted for welcoming Jesus into their lives.

Cut to the temple in Jerusalem 40 days later. An odd couple come shuffling out of the dark, coughing and wheezing and muttering to themselves. Oh oh, thinks Joe, better give them a wide berth, don't make eye contact whatever you do. But no, suddenly Anna and Simeon open up and everything changes, yet again strangers are telling Mary and Joe what's going on. More confirmation, more encouragement, that they are not mad. Those shepherds were telling the truth, Elizabeth was right. This is God's story, this is God's plan, and though there may be some long years of waiting up ahead, it has begun now.

Cut to the Jordan, 30 years later, and the same thing happens. John testifies that God's son is here. His cousin's baptism is the experience which shows John what is going on. And John, who let's face it is a good talker, passes on the news.

John announces to Jesus and those listening that he hadn't known exactly who would be the one, all that God had told him was this – you'll know when you see a dove come down on the man as a sign of the Holy Spirit. John knew that someone was coming, he'd been warning everyone, but he did not know who. So John does not know his cousin is the Messiah until he sees the dove land on him. After that you can't shut him up – he tells everyone, including Jesus. He confirms to his cousin what had been growing slowly inside of Jesus, the conviction of his calling. And John tells everyone listening so they can know it too. Until that moment only Jesus had carried that truth inside of him. Now, like Elizabeth with Mary, and the shepherds and Simeon and Anna with the new baby, other people, without being prompted, witness to the fact that Jesus is different and God is doing something new. This is why it's so vital. It's others recognising God's work when they see it and bearing witness to that fact. Later Jesus would often rely on others doing this as he went around teaching, seeming almost shy at times to tell others about himself. Instead he wrapped his pearls in parables and miracles, anecdotes and questions, and then he waited for others to recognise him. And speak it out.
Still the same today really.

All The Wrong Credentials

When Jesus told his story about the two brothers, the two parties, the famine, the pigs, the inheritance, the depression, the set-speech repentance and the crazy father, I wonder whether he realised it would go down in history as the number one 'top of the parables pops' story. If I had a pound for every time I've heard a talk in church about this I'd have £2354.73. In reality, when Jesus told this parable it was deeply shocking for a variety of reasons. This is a retelling of Jewish history, this is the story of Jacob and Esau retold, but instead of Jacob/Israel returning filthy rich, here the prodigal is coming home just plain filthy... and instead of the angry brother out looking for Jacob to take revenge, it's the compassionate father who's there waiting, with reconciliation in his hands.

There are many surprising things about this story, funny moments too, like the way the father runs to embrace his son at the end. Really??!! A dignified man getting all jaunty and over-excited, kicking up his heels and hurtling it down the road for his lost boy. Think of the Queen jumping out of a helicopter with James Bond in 2012, it's that startling, that comedic, that strange. Likewise at the beginning of the story the lad goes to his dad and says, 'Oh by the way, could you just give me all the money that's due to me when you're dead, like, right now, with no questions asked? Know what I mean?' And the father of course clips him round the ear and says, 'Don't be daft, lad. Is it April the 1st? Was I born yesterday? Are you havin' a laugh?' Except the father doesn't say that. He simply hands over the money!!! Like – what??? Really? Something there perhaps about the lives and gifts we've all been given, and the freedom we have to live them out, making our own choices, with or without the involvement of our heavenly father. What will we choose to do?

Cutting back to the famous scene where it's not the rich Jacob returning with wives and children, but the prodigal with a bad smell and a swarm of flies, what does that suggest? Perhaps this. Jesus's audience would have known well the Jacob version – the son returning with all the right credentials, having made a kind of success of things. So Jesus subverts that, offering this message – God isn't just on the side of Jacob and his like – but he's on the side of the filthy prodigals. The ones who have nothing to justify their place back home. The ones with all the wrong credentials. Those who don't look at all spiritual, those who don't dress right, those who have wasted the things they had. Anyone daring to limp home with a chaotic history and a hungry heart.

Sam and Paul

Reading the beginning of Sam Childers' book *Another Man's War* has really made me think about the different ways God uses people's gifts. Sam is a fearless man who goes where few others would dare. He rescues children and families from the brutal, bloodthirsty Lord's Resistance Army in Sudan and Uganda. Sam himself freely admits that he welcomes skirmishes with the L.R.A. as opportunities to take out more of their cruel fighters.

A couple of years back I read Paul Rusesabagina's book *An Ordinary Man* about the time when he rescued 1268 people from the murderous militia during the Rwandan Genocide of 1994. Members of the local militia came day after day to his hotel to slaughter those who had hidden there for refuge. Paul describes how he looked for the soft places inside the killers, appealing to their humanity and softening them up with kindness and gifts. Each day he was able to send them away without completing their killing.

Two very different men. Both peacemakers I would say. Both working for justice in this world.

Sam, a man whose own history and drug-dealing background is riddled with violent encounters, is not afraid to confront and destroy the forces of evil in his quest to bring hope and freedom and new life.

Paul, a great diplomat and negotiator, was not afraid to sit down and converse with the blood-spattered men who slaughtered so many others.

My initial instinct is to wonder which one is right and best, Paul the calming influence or Sam the gung-ho fighter? But considering both stories I have changed my thinking. There is nothing to compare. It seems to me that God uses different people with their different gifts, personalities and life experiences, and it's a waste of energy to somehow try and work out which way is best. It misses the point. God is diverse and uses people in drastically different ways.

I believe we are God's weapon of choice in this world. And not a Christian cardboard cut-out version of ourselves, but the real thing, our genuine selves, with our foibles, mistakes, weaknesses, strengths, doubts, fears, gifts and background. I certainly find that this is the story again and again in the Bible. Not gung-ho, squeaky clean heroes who have it all worked out, but diverse people who find themselves, sometimes in spite of themselves, changing the world a little bit, bringing peace, justice and compassion – the marks of the kingdom of God.

There's a great scene in the movie *Regarding Henry* which hits this nail on the head for me. Harrison Ford, not as Indiana Jones, but as Henry the broken lawyer, is trying to find his way in life after a debilitating accident. Bradley, the nurse who helped him get back on his feet, encourages him with his own story of a damaged past that somehow got turned around. Bradley used to play college football but had to give it up after his knees buckled during a game. He tells Henry he has bad knees, then tells him, 'Ask me if I mind having bad knees?' Before Henry can get the words out Bradley says, 'No. I don't. The therapist that helped me walk again – he was so cool that I thought, that's what I wanna do. Check it out. You're walking, you're talking, you're sitting here drinking some pretty expensive beer. I had something to do with that. If it weren't for my knees I'd never have met you. So I don't mind having bad knees.'

Bradley loved football, and his world surely fell apart with his injury. But now he dares to say that his experience has enabled him to help folks like Henry, to reach out and give them a new start. His own difficulties have become something he can offer others, to give them a new way forward.

Like Sam Childers and Paul Rusesabagina, Bradley is using who he is to help others. In the unique way only he can. I am both inspired and humbled by these kinds of stories. I'll never do anything that dramatic. But I hope, I pray, that I can use who I am and what I can do, the awkward, bumbling, sometimes inappropriate, shy person I am – the Dave Hopwood that God has made me to be – to help others.

Letter or Spirit?

During my time working at the Lee Abbey holiday and conference centre in north Devon we got into the habit of making a festive video each year to welcome our guests for the Christmas break. This was filmed in the woods, at the site where we felled each year's large Christmas tree. One year we planned to make the film on the second Sunday of December, but for various reasons we had to move the date of filming to the following week. I'm so glad we did. In the intervening seven days the weather changed, it snowed and the forest turned white. The result was magical and fitted the video perfectly.

Lee Abbey, like so much of the country that Christmas, was completely covered in snow. So much so that we were worried that our guests would not be able to turn up for their holiday. We gritted (our teeth and the road!) and the way through was just clear enough. It's an amazing setting, on the rugged Devon coast – beautiful at the best of times, but add a few feet of whiteness...

However, in spite of this massive duvet of snow it wasn't a white Christmas.

Nope.

You see there is a very important piece of criteria which makes it officially a white Christmas. Just a tiny, weeny, minuscule, microdot of a detail.

A single flake of snow has to fall from the sky on Christmas Day.

Yep.

The whole of the country can be strewn with abandoned cars, clogged snowploughs, giant snowmen and hurtling toboggans, but if a single flake of snow does not fall from the heavens on the big day itself then it's not a white Christmas. Even though it's white *at* Christmas. Bing could have dreamt all he wanted, his dreaming that year didn't come true. Technically.

Mad, isn't it? Bonkers, to use another technical term.

But then that's the difference between the letter of the law and the spirit of the law. The letter of the law is rigid, fixed, firm. Unforgiving you might say. I might walk out of my house and step into a ten foot snowdrift and freeze my tonsils off. But as far as the letter of the law is concerned...

I'm a *spirit of the law* man myself – can you tell?

The spirit of the law enables people to manoeuvre. It allows God (if it's possible to say this) to break his own rules. Because the law exists to serve man not man to serve the law. So you find the God who once outlined countless food laws (to aid the people's health and development) later overriding those laws in order to connect with people all over the world. You find the God behind the Law of Moses then breaking it in order to invade this world through an unmarried mother. You find him inciting the prophets to become ritually unclean and socially unacceptable to shock the locals into seeing what really mattered.

We are always tempted to become brittle and unmoving where laws and religions are concerned. It's safer.

But Christmas is about the God who does the opposite. Jesus described the work of God as being like the wind, something you cannot pin down, box or nail to a church noticeboard. This can be frustrating, because just as you feel you have hold of God, like a divine bar of soap he slips through your fingers. But then that's also why I believe he sent us a man to follow, not a rule book.

Spiritual Punk Rock

Watch any documentary about the punk music explosion in the late seventies and sooner or later I guarantee someone will say, 'When I saw the Sex Pistols I thought, if they can do it, I can have a go.'

One of the key aspects of the mad, raucous jamboree that was punk was this – anyone could join in. And plenty of people did. It was music of the people by the people for the people. Not everyone loved it of course and it soon imploded, but that wasn't the point. For the first time in music history it wasn't just about the talented few – it was about anyone.

I've often thought of prayer as the same kind of thing. A sort of spiritual anarchy. Anyone can have a go, you don't have to be good at it, and you can be raw, gritty, blunt and honest.

There are moments in the gospel blogs – John chapter 11 verse 41 and Matthew chapter 11 verse 25 – when Jesus explodes with his own wall-of-sound prayers. In public. It's not exactly 'Anarchy in Israel' -- but it may well have sounded like it. You see – most other people didn't pray like Jesus prayed. He said it like it was, he didn't put a religious spin on it, or use a holy kind of voice and archaic language. He spoke the language of the street, and he chatted to God as if he was right there next to him.

At times he tells God about his hopes, fears, faith and dreams. 'Father, if it's at all possible to rethink this plan, I'd be grateful. I don't want to do this,' he whispers in the gathering shadows of Gethsemane. 'My God – why have you let me down?!' he screams from the darkness of the cross. He doesn't hold back. Lets it all out. Spiritual punk rock.

And he wasn't the first. Read the book of psalms and you'll find a back catalogue of angry, gentle, repentant, desperate, hopeful songs. You can let it all out with God. One of the things I love about the film *Bruce Almighty* is that Bruce's relationship with God begins when he looks up to the heavens and lets out all his venom and frustration about the mess of his life.

It could be the case that everyone actually prays. Secretly. Perhaps we all utter our own forms of deep, guttural, heartfelt prayers, whatever our faith. These might well be expressed in sighs or groans, complaints or wisps of cigarette smoke rising like incense on the street corners. Cries for help, longings for something more, pleas for a better way. Ragged, half-formed snatches of conversation, unspoken communication, rising toward the unknown God.

If I'm honest my prayers in private are far more ragged and untidy than my prayers in public. In public I do my best to make my prayers sound like *The Hallelujah Chorus*, in private I often sound a little like Johnny Rotten.

I get distracted and forget the right words. I fumble for the meaning and repeat myself. I neglect to say Amen, then realise, backpedal and say it after the event. And of course many more of my prayers rise from the stress of my being, invisible fretful yawps rising into the ether, like hopeful, desperate smog. Our prayers may not be neat and tidy, but we are not invited to pray in that way. Jesus encouraged us to avoid praying as a show to impress others, and to speak to God honestly from our hearts. (See Matthew 6 verses 5-6.)

The Unimaginable

The other day we watched *Back to the Future part 2* with our daughter Amy.

We loved it and got well sucked in, but later something occurred to me. According to the movie, in the year 2015, people will have all kinds of weird and wonderful 'futuristic' things – videophones, flatscreen TVs with multiple channels, flying cars, jackets that adapt to your clothing size, and a hoverboard (which my daughter now wants).

Now some of these gadgets have turned up on time, though admittedly the hoverboards are little low-tech compared with Marty McFly's. But there was one huge omission in *Back to the Future part 2*. One thing that director Robert Zemeckis, producer Steven Spielberg and screenwriter Bob Gale just could not imagine back then in 1989. Something that now dominates our life but was totally absent from the movie. Arguably the most important invention since the printing press.

The double-yew double-yew double-yew.
The internet.

It's totally absent from the future as seen in their movie. They had no concept of this thing which I now use every day, hour by hour. This thing that has spawned YouTube, Facebook, Twitter, Snapchat, Instagram, Tinder, downloading, smartphones, e-books and iTunes. A global revolution. It's yet to come up with time travel, but hey! give it time, and we may not even need a Delorean.

We would all love to have more access to the future. Most magazines have horoscope pages; and bestselling paperbacks and DVDs predict what life may be like for us in the next ten, twenty, fifty years. Economists, prophets, musicians, poets, novelists and politicians all have their stabs at giving us a picture of what's around the corner. Curiosity, fear and the desire to control our destiny mean we sometimes pay good money for a vision of future things.

The writers of the Bible were like Bob Gale, Spielberg and Zemeckis. They predicted things about the future, imagined scenarios, had visions of how things might look. But they were rooted in their own time. They used language, images and references which are alien to us now. The most famous prophetic biblical book is Revelation. It's full of the kind of things you might find in a Spielberg movie – wars, plagues, strange creatures, signs in the sky, cosmic battles, desperate rescues, gleaming cities, heroes and villains. It used to scare the pants off me. Less so now because I realise that there are so many different theories about what it all means. Like Bob Gale, we cannot imagine some of the things referenced in it.

It's called apocalyptic – but apocalypse just means 'a revealing’ a 'lifting of the veil' – a disclosure of something. Not necessarily about the end of the world or vast destruction at all. All through history many predictions have been made based on this book, and so many have been wide of the mark. It seems that many people down the ages have thought that the age they were living in could well be the last one. What is often overlooked is that the main reason for recording the vision of the Revelation was to encourage those living through hard times that one day goodness and compassion will win through, justice will rise and the evil in the world will be wiped out forever. A message for 2000 years ago. A message for now.

One of the best predictions in the Old Testament is that a new king will rise. A leader who cares about people, a leader who will shun celebrity, money, fame and power. A prime minister who will not be in it for himself, but in it for us. Many prophets predicted this, although like Spielberg and Zemeckis, they only got a brief glimpse of this new future. (Have a look at Ezekiel 34 verses 11 to 16, or Daniel 7 verses 13 to 14.) We are fortunate, we can get a bigger picture. A widescreen, 3D experience. We have the four gospel blogs of Matthew, Mark, Luke and John. The accounts of the life of Jesus recorded by those who 'saw his glory'.

This is all a long way from wearing your trousers inside out and putting on two ties as they do in *Back to the Future part 2*. If nothing else that movie reminds me that none of us can clearly see the future and, as the apostle known as Paul once wrote, 'we now see [God and his ways] through a glass darkly,' or through a dirty window, with smudges and grease stains and fingerprints all over it. One day I believe we'll see clearly but until then I need a shedload of humility and integrity to admit that I am, to a large degree, guessing in the dark, guided by God's spirit, but limited in my visions and imaginings.

As for time travel, I'm afraid I'm a firm believer it'll never happen, with or without a Delorean. If it was ever invented, however far into the future, we would have already started meeting folks coming back to see us from there. That is, unless they are really, really good at keeping it a secret. In which case, your dog may really be called Einstein and have come in a Skoda from 3015.

Freedom and Responsibility

About ninety percent of the Bible is storytelling. Something like that anyway. All kinds of mysteries and adventures unravel on the pages and we are invited to find ourselves in those tales of the unexpected. Take the beginning as an example. It's very easy to miss the big story as we chew on what our particular standpoint is about the age of the earth, and what seven days means and whether Eve made an apple pie or a rhubarb crumble. Personally I think it was probably sprouts that made the earth fall into chaos and disruption, but there you go. (Sprouts still have that power to this day.) Ultimately, we are led into this epic tale of a cosmos created by a God who speaks and breathes over the chaos. He carefully designs, and interacts with the work of his hands. Then horror! Evil seeps into the beauty and the splendour, causing deceit and decay. The end is nigh so soon! Or is it?

Early on, a couple of huge themes, very relevant themes, are celebrated in the Bible. God gives to people a couple of extraordinary gifts for their time on the planet. Freedom and responsibility. Towards the end of the first chapter of the Genesis blog we're told that God makes people (implying that people are carefully crafted and highly valued) and then he gives them the earth so they can look after it. They are called to 'be masters of it' and to 'subdue it' – but that doesn't mean just 'suck it dry for all it's worth'. They are asked to be good bosses. Good bosses are well loved and respected by their employees. Good bosses can save people in a time of crisis. Good bosses set the best interests of others first.

In the second post of the Genesis blog the man is asked to name the animals. He has the freedom to do what he likes here. If he wants to call an elephant a radiator he can do it. A hamster can be a 'puff-cheeked, nut cruncher' if he likes, and I have it on good authority that his original name for a cat was 'Oy! that's my chair you're sitting on'. To this day the gift of animal naming goes on. We once had a guinea pig called Theo. You may have a dog called Rover. Or Fido. Or Deefor. Or a couple of goldfish called Ness'n'Dorma. But I digress, back to the story.

So people get a brand new world and they can do what they like with it. But they are invited to be responsible with it and make the best of it. To work with it, develop it, celebrate it. To be the kind of bosses that set the interests of others high on their agenda. Freedom and responsibility. Two great and generous gifts. I sit here now listening to Nessun Dorma on YouTube (I googled it to find out the spelling for that previous goldfish joke) and I'm reminded of those gifts and appreciate them once again.

One of the really heartening and encouraging things in life is to see people exercising those gifts to make the world a better, kinder place. Those who realise the need for toilets for those who have none, and so invent the idea of *Toilet Twinning*. The artist McCrow who came up with the idea of making the world safer with *One Less Gun*, taking dangerous weapons, painting them and transforming them into works of art. The businessmen who set up free universities for those who would not normally be able to afford education. The folks who enable us to send shoe boxes full of Christmas toys halfway round the world. The people who set up Change.org, offering a website where others may campaign for truth, freedom and justice.

These, and so many other initiatives of imagination and generosity, seem to me to flow from those gifts of freedom and responsibility. Expressions of the gifts God has given us. Admittedly the newspapers are full of examples of the misuse of these precious gifts, but there are so many examples of the opposite. Many more than we will ever know. Whether that devastating fall turned up via apple pie, rhubarb crumble or sprout quiche, there is still space in the world to buck the trend and make things better, not worse.

They'll Never Get Their Heads Round That!

Sometimes it bugs me the way we complicate the faith. Take the word *Trinity* for starters. For aeons we have been challenged to explain the God who is three in one, the *Trinity*, and yet the Bible never uses this word. We've made a rod for our own backs and we keep getting beaten over the head with it, to confuse the metaphor. What the Bible does say from the very outset is that God is word, God is spirit and God is being.

If I showed you a poster for the movie *The Dark Knight* would it be a picture of Batman, Christian Bale or Chris Nolan's epic movie? Well of course it's all three. You can argue for one in particular but that's how pictures work, on many levels. One poster, many images. The Bible is a picture of the indefinable God. Time and again we find this. The spirit, word and being of God keep breaking into the restrictions of this world, breaking into the small confines of our minds and lives.

The spirit of God hovered over nothing and made it into something, not a surprise really. The ultimate creator creates something. God spoke and things happened – the word of God went out and got busy. And God walks in the creation he has made, communicating with people like us. God is being, God is word, God is spirit. The challenge then is not to explain it but to weave that into our lives. What does it mean for me that God exists in those terms? What does it mean for me today in the ordinary nature of my life?

It's a tough call to resist the temptation to try and explain God. To live with a God who is ultimately way beyond my own reasoning. This computer may be impressive – but it can't do the washing up. I can try typing in the command but

I doubt that it will shuffle off the desk and start running the tap. It's not hardwired in that way. So too we cannot get our heads around everything in the universe. We love science and technology and philosophy, but these will always be limited tools in our hands. God is mystery, life is mystery, and our daily existence is often that too.

In his book *Searching for God Knows What* Don Miller writes about us losing the beauty and the mystery in our relationship with God. He writes about the way much of the Bible is written in poetry because it's all relational. And sometimes we're reading verses to think 'so this is what I need to do' or 'this is how to be right with God' when actually we need to read it as it is, just to know the character of God.

I was recently part of a conversation where a friend Steph was encouraging us to listen to God, not because we want him to tell us something specific, but just because he *is*. We may hear nothing, but he is in that silence. When we listen to others we give them value. By listening to God we do the same. Not easy to do though when we are restless for results.

Perhaps that's why the notion of trinity continues to vex and fascinate us. We are invited to sit with it, walk with it, let it seep into our lives. Not work it out or explain it. We may wrestle with this all our lives, and only have brief moments of surrendering to the mystery of God. But those fleeting glimpses could be gold dust. I wonder if one day God woke up and thought, 'How can I impress upon people that I am not like them? I know, got it! I'll be three ***and*** one – 'cause they'll never get their heads round that.'

All That Jazz

Jazz may just be the best musical representation of my relationship with God. I recently went to a concert of modern jazz and part way through that thought hit me. You see I struggle with modern jazz, I'm a sort of two verses, a bridge and an oft-repeated, catchy chorus kind of guy. Plus I'm no musician and I love words. So listening to this concert I was a little lost at times, only occasionally aware of hooks and brief snatches of melody as pieces came and went. It was brilliantly performed, and I could appreciate the skill and musical craftsmanship, but I felt in the dark a little, standing at a distance, admiring from afar. Occasionally getting a little focus.

But that is like God for me too. He is beyond me, different, ungraspable, I can't pin him down to a few verses and a catchy chorus. And so it should be. I'm small, fickle, gritty and dusty, wayward and frequently tripping over my own feet, when I'm not putting them firmly in my mouth. God is not like that. I can appreciate and wonder at his skill, craftsmanship, endless compassion, and fiery passion for justice. I can see his hands in the work of others, see his smile on the faces of friends and strangers, and hear his laughter and tears when moments of joy and sorrow erupt amongst us. But I am standing at a distance, only occasionally catching glimpses, grabbing at brief hooks and melodies. I know he has come close in Jesus, and I have been brought into a new world as a result. But I am forever the prodigal, rushing home, yet again covered in pigswill and dung, after anther misadventure. And it's not long before I'm dashing off again a few days later, with another bag packed, on escapades of my own making.

So the music plays on, consistent, but unpredictable, beautiful but in another language. A language I am just beginning to grasp. The notes rise and fall and the rhythms come in and out. And I am fortunate to be a part of it, listening, wondering, sometimes perplexed, and occasionally drawn in, tapping my feet, and taken to another place.

One day, St Paul once wrote, we will grasp it all, but for now we hear snatches of this and that, we tune in and we tune out. And we are grateful for the Great Jazz Musician who is opening our ears little by little to his chords and breaks and riffs and scales, through the humble, profound work of his tireless spirit, and the sacrificial dedication of his son Jesus.

50 Shades of Grace

Depending on where you get your information, men think about sex every six or eight seconds. Either way, it's a lot. So if you're chatting to a guy and he phases out for a moment... you get the picture. Which is probably why the writers of the Bible use sex as a metaphor an awful lot. Something we don't tend to do very much nowadays.

Way before *50 Shades of Magnolia* appeared, King Solomon wrote his own erotic diary, detailing the er... ups and downs of his love life. Not one known for being coy he named it *The Song of* well... *Solomon*. A sort of 'Confessions of a king with 700 wives and 300 concubines' kind of novel. Nowadays it's seen as a sort of parable, a metaphor about God's passionate love for people – but hey – it's an awfully erotic one, chock full of ripe pomegranates and gardens of spices. Nudge nudge. Wink wink.

In her own book, the gorgeous Esther joins King Xerxes' harem, and we're told that she 'pleased the king' more than all the other women. In other words, she was a great lover. She was so pleasing Xerxes made her Queen, and she was perfectly placed to then rescue her people from a murderous, racist plot. My theory is this – when she approached the king without an invitation he was unlikely to dispose of her, knowing how good she was in the bedroom. I might be wrong, but I can't help thinking that the God who created bodies perfectly understands the power of these things.

When people give up on God they are regularly described in biblical terms as prostituting themselves, or to use another contemporary term, they turn into rent boys. Hiring themselves out for sex, or even paying others to become their new sex partners. Shocking really, isn't it? The books of Hosea and Ezekiel both feature this kind of behaviour.

Ezekiel tells a lengthy story in chapter 16 of his book, which features sex and gore. He describes rescuing a baby left dying in a field, squirming in its own blood. The baby grows up into a beautiful woman, but she then takes off, gives up on her true lover, and plays the tart, grabbing sex from anyone who'll do the business for her. Later, in chapter 23, Ezekiel tells a similar story about two sisters, who run off looking for lovers they can pay for sex. The older is then murdered by her 'lovers'. The younger sister completely loses the plot. Both stories are illustrations of the way people can start well with God, then give up on the relationship and sell out to other things and people. Both are shocking, graphic, tawdry tales of lust. And though the stories are about women – the metaphor applies to both sexes.

Hosea doesn't just tell a tale of wayward sex, he lives one. He marries his wife, who then takes other lovers, even paying some of them for sex. Chapter three of this dark story sees Hosea tramping through the night to find his wife in another man's bed, dragging her from his arms and taking her home. And his message to her? He says, 'You won't be having any sex at all for a while, not with me, or anyone. And that'll be a sign to the people round here that they have lost their precious, intimate relationship with their God.' I can't help wondering how he got this message to the rest of the neighbourhood. Did he nail a note to the church noticeboard? 'Me and my wife aren't doing it at the moment because you and God aren't doing it.' In all these graphic encounters the message remains the same. The hero, the devoted lover, wants to rescue the wayward people from their tawdry, destructive ways.

When Jesus turns up he describes himself as the bridegroom, another relationship reference. Drawing on the image of a guy who invites people to a big celebration of a healthy joining-together – with wine, food, dancing, family, friends, promises and a hopeful view of the future. This image of a bride and groom then continues to reoccur throughout the New Testament. Prostitutes feature a lot too, we're told Jesus spent a lot of time with whores and lost men and women. These were the very people who were close to the kingdom of God, he said, way ahead of the religious experts.

The writers of the Good Book were clearly not embarrassed about sex references. The books of Proverbs, Isaiah, Micah and Joel also feature them. In chapter 2 of his biblical blog Jeremiah even goes so far as to liken the rebellious to camels on heat and donkeys sniffing after the next available mate. Not very Anglican! Maybe the biblical writers used sex as a metaphor because people were obsessed with sex back then, whereas nowadays we're... oh... just the same. Maybe we're missing a *trick* here. (Pun intended.)

Faith Value

I went for a walk the other evening in the amazing Valley of Rocks, not far from our house. The sun was setting over the bay and the setting was just perfect. On the way I was thinking about how we're all people of philosophies and beliefs. I mean, the Valley of Rocks to me is an amazing example of the glory of God. It's staggering beauty reminds me of God's creativity and presence in the universe. This is because I believe certain things when I walk through that valley. I bring a vision as I go. I can't help it. But I know that others believe plenty of other things when they go through that valley. It seems to me that whether we are Methodist, Buddhist, Atheist or a Trekkie (or all four) it's because we believe things about the world, people and life, and about the past and the future. We have formed an outlook, a world-view, a system of beliefs about the world and the way it works. I reckon that to be human is to believe things. At the risk of sounding heretical, very little can really be proved. Even scientific fact. I heard Brian Cox on the radio a while back saying there are not really any facts – just theories that haven't yet been disproved. And whether I think the Valley of Rocks was made by the hand of a creator, or forged by the process of evolution, it's all faith. I think we have been designed like that. To put our faith in things.

The biblical take on faith is this – 'It is the confident assurance that what we hope for is going to happen. It is the evidence of things we cannot yet see.' So says the writer of Hebrews, at the beginning of chapter 11 of his biblical email.
So to believe in anything – a business plan, a relationship, a sporting team or ability, life priorities, the love of another person – all these things come down to our faith and where we place it. I cannot prove the world was made by God but

then no one can prove that it was a freak of nature. Theories and ideologies can be presented but then we must choose where to place our trust. Ultimately I suppose it's about meaning. We believe in things because they give us purpose and pleasure and direction. The reason the writers of the Bible bash on and on about the world being designed by a caring creator, was to remind folks that they are not an accident. That people matter. That the God of the Bible was not like the tyrannical gods of the time who demanded you burn your crops and sacrifice your children in order to please them. No, said the biblical writers, God is not like that. He is not barbaric and brutal, churlish and demanding. He is creative and caring and waiting to be discovered.

References to this creator God pop up all over the Bible, in the Old Testament and the New. Often when a crisis was looming. The people and their prophets kept returning in catastrophe to the bottom line, this world is not an accident, and neither are the people in it. It may be damaged and chaotic and full of destruction at times, but there is more going on, an unseen reality. An unseen kingdom. And for me, evenings like that one in the Valley of Rocks are timely reminders of that. Nourishing and heartening glimpses.

Happy Are the Unhappy

For years the bit of the Bible we call the Beatitudes completely flummoxed me.

Jesus sits on the side of a mountain one day and, looking a lot like Moses, he produces a whole load of new commandments. His speech includes this –

'Happy are those who are poor, for the Kingdom of God is given to you.
Happy are those who are hungry now, for you will be satisfied.
God blesses you who weep now, for the time will come when you will laugh with joy.
God blesses you who are hated and excluded and mocked and cursed because you are identified with me, the Son of Man.' (Luke chapter 5)

As someone once said, it almost reads like 'happy are the unhappy'! Blessed are the cursed... strange eh?
However, more recently a couple of things have helped me see the bigger picture here.

Firstly the context. Jesus lived in a time when most people figured that if you were poor, grieving, pushed down or hungry, then you had probably brought it on yourself. It was some kind of punishment, some sign that God was unhappy with you. A curse. So Jesus is correcting this – he is saying that God is with you when your life falls apart. It is not a punishment, these things happen. Life gets hard, it ambushes you. But God is with you, and sometimes more tangibly so, when things go wrong. In fact, the phrase 'Blessed are...' or 'Happy are...' can also be translated 'God is with...'

'God is with the poor, the lowly, the persecuted, the hungry.'

Jesus follows this by saying watch out if you're rich, satisfied and prosperous. These things don't necessarily mean God is with you. Riches or poverty are not a sign of God's presence. And we know that affluence can dull us to the things of God sometimes. Abundance can bring its own stresses, and even build a wall between us and God.

These were shocking words to the people of his day, and the attitude that prevailed. The people had been programmed to think that sickness and loss indicated God's curse, and Jesus spends much of his time challenging this idea. Right up to the point where he himself becomes poor, broken-hearted, rejected, grieving, persecuted and dying. And in doing so finally upends the curse and truly blesses the world.

The other thought about the Beatitudes is this. It's a mission statement. God has come out of the closet, showing his true colours. Why are the poor blessed? Why should those who mourn be happy? Why will the broken-hearted laugh out loud? Because Jesus is here, God's in town, and he's going to spend most of his time with them, showing them that even in their distress and trauma they matter to God. Let the 'haves' glory in their wealth if that's what they want, God will be with the 'don't haves'. Jesus went on to spend the following three years living out these words. Spending his time with those in pain and need. And that's when many of the 'cursed' found blessing.

Matthew also recorded his version of the Beatitudes in his blog, chapter 5, and it's worth noting that he remembers Jesus saying 'blessed are the spiritually poor'. Luke, who has an eye for the outsiders, records, 'blessed are the poor.' I think Matthew took note of the blessing for the spiritually poor, the 'not very spiritual' folk, because that's how he felt. He had been a collaborator working with the Romans, a despised tax collector, a corrupt banker of his day. He was also a party animal, and his way of celebrating his new start with Jesus was to throw a big shindig, inviting his mates along who were mostly other tax collectors, sinners and prostitutes. I guess he didn't feel very spiritual really. So he found hope in Jesus, who went looking for types like him. And he's the patron saint for the rest of us. Those who too are spiritually poor. We're blessed. Jesus is in town for us.

A Life of Contradiction

The problem with God is he is what you might call *different*, i.e. not us. And as a result, it seems to me, we all end up reducing him down. Whatever our religion or whether we claim to have faith or not, we reduce God down to our ideas of existence or non-existence. And to believe in something more, something higher, something other than this life, in this age, in this culture, means we all end up with lives of contradiction. We may believe in peace and truth and hope and kindness, but we can often be aggressive, false, despairing and unkind. And very sadly this is sometimes as a result of the faith we or others hold.

We find it hard to get over ourselves. We are stuck with our humanity. And it seems naive in the light of this to say we believe in things mystical, things of faith, things unprovable, things unseen. And the precious gift of faith (whatever we place it in, God, people, abilities, relationships) can become a weapon, a razorblade wielded to prove others wrong and ourselves right. We become dogmatic and brittle, rather than compassionate and understanding.

A while ago I came across a photograph of an unusual piece of art, a real cloud in the middle of a room, created by artist Berndnaut Smilde. It put me in mind of the image of God in the desert, described in the book of Exodus as 'a pillar of cloud'. Uncontainable, non-boxable, uncontrollable. Also a while back I read a book called *This Thirtysomething Life* by Jon Rance, a sort of male Bridget Jones kind of thing, full of revealing insights about what it is to be a guy in his thirties approaching fatherhood, with all his fears, desires, hopes, madness and junk food. I especially enjoyed his highly unhealthy snacks, eaten mostly in his shed.

There's a moment in the book when Harry attends his beloved granddad's funeral, and whilst admitting at this point that he is an atheist and does not believe in any kind of afterlife (which makes the loss of his granddad all the more difficult) he hopes he is proved wrong, and hopes his cheeky grandfather is looking down on him from somewhere. It leapt out at me as a profound moment of humanity in the book. For some it is just too difficult to believe in something more, in a God who is 'other', perhaps in the light of a world full of trouble and hypocrisy. And yet there is still the cry of the soul, the yelp of humanity, the barbaric yawp (as Robin Williams puts it in *Dead Poets Society*) – that reaches for something more.

Author David Runcorn describes the way we reduce Jesus to our own terms and ideas in his book *Choice, Desire and the Will of God: What More Do You Want?* In an ancient culture of scapegoats (a culture of blame if you like) Jesus becomes the ultimate scapegoat. Scapegoats were animals upon which was dumped all the troubles and mistakes, wrongdoing and crimes. This unsuspecting, beleaguered goat was sent away, symbolically removing that burden from people. We of course continue with our own culture of blame, and every day scapegoats appear in our papers, and on our tablet and TV screens. We do our best to dump our guilt and disease on them, attempting to feel better about ourselves.

Nowadays if anything goes wrong one of the first questions asked is – 'Who can we blame?' Scapegoat culture. Who can we dump all this on so we don't have to face the same mistakes and crimes within our lives? To this thinking Jesus is a problem and a solution. He is a problem because he highlights the very fact that, if we dare face up to it, we are all to blame, shifting it onto others is only a way of hiding from ourselves. So he shines a light on each one of us. 'It isn't what you eat, drink, watch, listen to, wear, or consume that corrupts you so much as what comes out of you towards the world and others,' he says. And to this he provides a strange, violent, unfathomable solution. He becomes a new kind of scapegoat to end all scapegoats. Requiring not perfection and goodness from us, but trust, and the embarking on a new kind of adventure.

When the people crossing the desert were bitten by poisonous snakes, in Numbers chapter 21, Moses was instructed by God to make a bronze image of one of those poisonous snakes and to hold it up on a pole. Moses then advised the sick people to trust God for healing and to express that trust by looking towards the image of the snake. Any who did this found themselves hunky-dory once again. When Jesus predicted his own death, in John chapter 3, it was this image that he used. Just as the bronze snake was a representation of the poison in their midst, so Jesus would become a sinful scapegoat, dying a criminal's death, a representation of the poison affecting the people. An image of the destructive danger within all our lives. He, like Moses, invited everyone to look towards that image as an expression of trust in God. A means of finding a new life, and a fresh start. A way of reconciling our lives of contradiction.

Culture Clash

It's 1977 and there is revolution in the air. It's the Queen's Silver Jubilee year and to celebrate a certain band brings out their version of *God Save The Queen*. Things may never be the same again.

I caught some clips from Top of the Pops in 1977 and it made me realise why Punk and New Wave caused such a stir in the late 70s. Top of the Pops was done in a certain way, with a particular look, a particular way of dancing, presented in a particular tone of voice. And apparently millions watched. I did anyway. The likes of Leo Sayer, Showaddywaddy, Pan's People and Manhattan Transfer, kept us glued to that goggle box on a Thursday night.

Cut to The Jam, on the same programme, with their debut single *In the City* – and suddenly we're talking something very different. Different attitude, different language, different style of presentation, different way of approaching things altogether.

Paul Weller and his mates were not dancing the same way, not singing the same way, they had anger and passion and they cared about their lyrics. They were tired of the old ways and they were out there to make something contrary happen. When you compare the two styles you can see why this new attitude was so revolutionary, the scene was set for a battle between the old and the new.

Cut to Lent and we find some similarities. Jesus was in a time of change, he was moving from being the local builder-carpenter who could fix your house and mend that table, to being a radical teacher who would shake the world to its absolute core. He was not going to dance, sing, act or speak in quite the same way as anyone else, and that required preparation. He was changing, and he needed 40 days alone to do that. To face himself, sort out his priorities and get well-grounded. He was about to make something different happen. A *new wave* kind of challenge to the way people lived, a *punk* explosion to their understanding of life. A different attitude, different language, a different way of being entirely. Passion, anger and energy. Something very different was coming about in that wilderness.

There was a strange and glorious moment on Top of the Pops when dancers Legs & Co (successors to Pans People) danced to *Bankrobber* by The Clash. In their own inimitable style. The Clash refused to appear on Top of the Pops so with their single riding high in the top 20 something had to be done. Enter Legs and Co dressed as er... yes... bank robbers, complete with stripy shirts, hankies over their faces and swag bags. It's a great example of the old and the new mixing together. A strange combination. Not at all in the spirit of punk. *Clashing*, you might say.

Jesus commented on this kind of thing, using wine skins and clothes as examples. He said something along the lines of, 'Trying to bring in the new can be tricky and awkward, it can result in a strange and unsettling mix that often makes a mess. People prefer the old to the new,' he said, 'so they try and hang on to bits of both, but trying to put the two together can cause accidents.'

People prefer the old to the new... change can be a challenge for all of us.

You Were Fitter in Your Facebook Picture

Lent is a celebration for our time. In these days when so many of us feel very pressured and stressed by the need to 'look' right and follow 'celebrity style' Jesus shows us there are other ways to tap into what really matters. He swapped all that kind of thing for 40 days in his desert boot camp, and I guess he must have looked pretty rough on some days; with no mirrors, make-up or airbrushing to be had. Just him and some rocks and a few wild animals. But boy, he tapped into the real stuff, the things that matter. Identity, purpose, patience, endurance and self-worth. These would serve him well in the mad days ahead. I wonder what Jesus would have posted on Facebook (or more likely Facescroll) during his 40 days. How about...

Day 1: Hungry.

Day 2: Hungry.

Day 3: Could murder a Yorkie.

Day 4. Still still still still hungry.

Day 5: Realllllllyyyy hungry.

Day 6: Reeeeeeeeaaaaalllllllllllllllyyyyyyyyyyyyyyyyyyyyyy
yyyyyyyy hungry.

Day 7: Battled with idolatry today. (Still hungry though)

Day 8: Battled with the abuse of power today. (Still hungry)

Day 9: Battled with the avoidance of pain today. (Still you-know-what)

Day 10: Those rocks look tasty.

Day 11: Just updated my profile picture, think I've lost a bit of weight...

You could argue that Henry the 8th was the first person to employ a little airbrushing when he got the painter Holbein to do the royal portrait. Henry has gone down in history as a fine figure of a man with strong sleek legs. In reality, by the time he was painted, his legs were heavily bandaged, and he was carrying a lot of extra weight. Once a keen sportsman, he had been injured and could no longer go jogging or jousting, he could still eat though. For England. And he did. Which meant that he rather resembled the Michelin Man. So he got Holbein to knock up a fantasy picture of him, and incredibly, that's how we remember the great Harry. Looking strong and dapper.

Unlike Jesus. The image of the man from Nazareth that has gone down in history is one of him looking shameful and bloody, murdered on an executioner's cross. The band Scouting for Girls once recorded a song called *You were fitter in your myspace picture*, it was about the disappointment of meeting someone in the flesh after viewing them online. I guess Jesus would have looked pretty rough after his days in the desert. He'd have probably been easily dismissed as he limped back into town that day. But boy, was he ready to take on the world. He didn't look like a celebrity one bit. But he was a prize fighter on the inside, tuned up for three years that would change history forever.

Lent: What Is It Good For?

Having spent the last few weeks chewing on Jesus's time in the wilderness, hoovering up bits of information about the experience, I've gathered a smörgåsbord of hunches and ideas on the subject. So here are a few.

Overall it seems to me that Jesus's time in the Judean desert covered things like:
The use and abuse of power, the avoidance of pain, idolatry and priorities, being grounded in reality, making friends with the desert, connecting with the old heroes and preparing for a colossal time of change.
There are, I'm sure, many other things going on but I'll just stick with these for now.

First a question – if you could morph stones into food, what would you make? Doughnuts? Roast beef and Yorkshire pudding? Curry? Tripe? Cream cakes? Chocolate? Marmite and liquorice sandwiches? To get an immediate connection with the food temptation just imagine what would be irresistible to you, and bear in mind that you have the power to make it happen.

Manna
I've discovered there is a flip side to this story. Many think of Lent as a time to 'give things up' but Jesus's quote about 'Man shall not live by bread but by the word of God' comes from a story about provision of food, not withholding it. It goes back to Deuteronomy (chapter 8 verse 3) and Moses retelling the events of the days in the desert when manna fell from the sky. Manna by the way means 'What is it?' It's one of those biblical jokes. The bread falls from the sky and people go, 'What is it?' And Moses says, 'Yes. What is it.' That's what we're asking,' say the people, 'what is it?'

'Exactly,' says Moses. 'Eh? What is it?' say the people. 'You got it,' says Moses. 'Yea, we got it,' say the people, 'but what is it?' 'Totally,' says Moses, 'what is it.' 'That's what we're asking – for goodness sake! What is it?' 'I told you – what is it.' 'Exactly – what is it??' 'Yes!!! It's what is it!! That's what it is!!!' And so it was called – 'What is it?' Which is what manna means. It's a bit like the Abbot and Costello baseball joke from the movie *The Naughty Nineties* about, 'Who's on first, What's on second, I don't know who's on third.'

But the point of manna was that the people got hungry and God provided what they needed. So food was supposed to point them to the food provider, the divine breadmaker. Whenever they ate they would remember the one who gave it to them. So – back to the question, what's your favourite food? Because whatever it is, it can remind you of the God who is behind everything, including your favourite food, or at least the ingredients of it. It's not about food *or* God, it's a case of food *and* God. Food can lead us to God. Not unlike the bread and wine at communion, we need food and drink, and we need God.

We think of the quote about 'man shall not live by bread alone' often as being about not needing things, but originally, in the desert in Deuteronomy, the people's need of bread was supposed to remind them of the one who gave them food, the divine breadmaker. 'You had no bread or wine or other strong drink, but he gave you food so you would know that he is the LORD your God.' [Deut 29 and also Deut 8.] He allowed them to get hungry so he could then provide for them, to encourage them to look to him for help and provision and not just be self-sufficient. Our need of food reminds us that there is someone who invented it. Like bread and wine reminding us of the God with us... We need bread and we need God.

The Use and Abuse of Power

Later Jesus would make bread from nothing, he would do the miracle then, when it was about having compassion on thousands of others. But he would not play power games, he would not magic up bread just to prove a point and satisfy his audience. Jesus had faced the temptation to lord it over others and he faced that down. If Jesus has a superpower then it is all about serving, he is powerful because he cares and kneels in the dust to wash feet. He would however use his bread-making power to deliver a sign – Isaiah chapter 25 verse 6 paints a picture of a God who lays on a feast for his people. Here is a feast of bread from a man who's starting to look a lot like the Messiah. Which brings us nicely on to impressions.

Doing impressions

Any Michael Caine impersonators out there?

Jesus's best qualifications were his impressions. In the wilderness he looks a little like Noah, who went into a boat for 40 days, a bit like Elijah who went into a desert and was helped by angels, and a lot like Moses who came face to face with idolatry, testing God, and bread from heaven. Jesus would continue to impersonate Moses and reference many other old heroes, (Abraham, Joshua, Daniel, Elisha, Isaiah) it was a vital tool for him as he wooed the people to trust him as a man of God. Actually it was nothing new, Joshua himself, needing to grab the people's respect and attention after the death of Moses, impersonated his predecessor by doing the biggest Mosaic miracle of all – splitting water in two. Crossing the Jordan was nowhere near as difficult as crossing the Red Sea, but Joshua needed to show folks he came from the same stock and was the next man from God. So parting water was his best shot. It worked.

Grounded

Jesus's time in the desert served him well – it grounded him so that when the fame and adulation came he was not overwhelmed or fazed by it... So often now people are thrust into the limelight and we read of their lives collapsing in on them. Jesus's time in the desert enabled him to keep his feet on the ground so that when the X Factor moments came he was not deceived by the lure of fame and the roar of the crowd. He saw failure and success as the impostors they are. He was not out to prove himself in any way. He was at peace with himself, he had made that peace in the long lonely days in the wilderness.

One of the things it has made me think is that perhaps Jesus made friends with the wilderness during his time there. Perhaps to some degree it became familiar, a known place, because he often returns to lonely wilderness places in times of stress, e.g. when John is murdered. Nick Baines also points out that Jesus went into the desert to face himself, which I also like. The place of emptiness where all else falls away. There is a phrase used in therapy – 'Wherever you go, there you are.' So many people fall apart when fame and adulation hits them, I wonder whether Jesus's answer to those clamouring voices that came later, was his time of preparation spent in the wilderness. He was, if you like, well grounded by the experience.

Ch...ch...ch...changes

When punk came along in 1977 it blew the old order of pop music right out of the water. The happy, soft-focused, gently swaying bands on Top of the Pops were not sure what to make of the likes of The Jam, The Stranglers and The Rods.

Other rocking giants of the airwaves went a little quiet for a while, waiting for the filth and the fury to go away. These new punks on the block did not sing, dance, act or behave in a way anyone else had quite known before. They were challenging the old order and bringing in a new time.

As was Jesus. His time in the desert prepared him for the massive changes ahead. He was moving from being the local carpenter-builder to being a radical, sometimes shocking, blast of a Messiah. Not just a new teacher, but a man who would live totally differently to anyone who had ever lived before. That would mean changes for the world around too. He was calling people to behave and act in a totally radical way. The old order would be shaken to its core. No one had quite seen anything like this. It would be a shock for a lot of people. In the desert Jesus prepared himself for all that these kind of changes would usher in.

Frankly My Dear, I Don't Give a D**n

There was a time when a line like the title above would make the censor's heart miss a beat. When Rhett Butler uttered his putdown at the end of *Gone With the Wind*, the censor cried, 'Cut!' The director agreed then left it in anyway.

Nowadays we don't bat an eyelid. We don't give a whotsit about an actor not giving a damn about something. Frankly my dear, it's the mildest thing you'll hear. I love films, I watch a lot of them, and I make reference to them when I speak, using them as launching pads for biblical stories. But I'm aware that many films these days are laden with expletives. As a Christian it unsettles me, and as a writer it irks me. Back in those *Gone With the Wind* days no one needed to say effin' this and jeffin' that. Anger, passion, humour and frustration were expressed without the requirement of anything beginning with f, s or c. So why is it necessary today? It's often referred to as *strong* language, but it seems to me to be weak, rather than strong language. Dialogue need not be peppered with it to make expression powerful.

The truth of course is that most folk don't notice it. It's not a problem. But I notice it. And I sometimes think twice before recommending films, if I know they are peppered with expletives. There were quite a few movies that I would have liked my parents to see, but could not recommend to them because I was aware of the language and knew it would get in the way of their enjoyment. I grew up in a household where I never heard my mum swear at all and only ever heard my dad swear once.

Jesus once advised folks to 'Let their yes be yes and their no be no, and their maybe be maybe…' Okay I added the last bit.

But his point was that there was no need to add other expressions to press home the point. Perhaps it's a bit like saying something was 'really perfect'. How can it be *really* perfect? Perfect is perfect. It's enough. I'm not in any way wishing to appear holy here, so apologies if this is coming across in that way. I say all kinds of things I shouldn't. But there's something about 'the silver screen' which enlarges, and perhaps approves of, behaviour. So when our heroes, or sympathetic villains, are foul-mouthed I take that on board. I absorb it. It shapes me.

Another frustration for me is the lack of creativity. To simply say the eff word a hundred times does not convey much and has little or no shock value. I am currently reading an historical novel, *The Devil's Chalice* by DK Wilson, and one of the striking things about their dialogue is the creative language used for insults and put downs. 'Hasty-witted manikin' and 'peevish fellow' come to mind. And there are dozens more. Perhaps we could be more imaginative, for example, not giving a flying *frappucino* about something. Years ago a friend and I thought that the word *window*, might be quite expressive for a put down. As in 'you're a right window.' The W allows for a certain amount of feeling in there.

All of this flies in the face of Paul's plea in his email to the Philippians, chapter 4 verse 8, to think on things that are pure, lovely, noble and admirable. That's the real nub of the issue I suppose. Films are full of conflict, and that's expressed in the dialogue. That's what makes a story interesting. But we don't live in a movie, we seek to inhabit a place once graced by the Prince of Peace. Who did admittedly once call the Pharisees a bunch of white-washed tombs and filthy bits of crockery, challenging them to clean up what was on the inside rather than worry about looking good. Perhaps that was the difference here, Jesus was using strong language to open a door, not merely polluting the place by distributing putdowns like discarded dog-poo bags. But cutting to the heart of problems and issues in such a way as to wake up those who needed help.

What is noticeable is that, in the darkest of moments, in the gravest of pain, under the greatest stress, what Jesus utters is not profanity, but profound prayers. 'Father, forgive them, for they don't know what they are doing.' 'My God, why have you abandoned me?' 'Into your hands I commit my spirit.'

Rock Bottom

In the week before Easter, the days we now call Holy Week, there was party/rebellion/betrayal/freedom/confusion in the air. Pilate was in Jerusalem because any big festival was always a dangerous time. There was always the chance of an uprising when the place was jammed with Passover pilgrims, and any suggestion of a Messiah in the neighbourhood could only exacerbate that.

So Jesus hides out with his friends in Bethany. Lies low to avoid arrest and does his best to warn his followers about what's coming. He predicts betrayal and cowardice on their part, and offers them coded references about resurrection.
Then, for the Passover, he sends a couple of them out to find a secret location, one he has pre-arranged for their final meal together. It’s cloak and dagger stuff with the kind of secret messages you might find between spies in a Bond movie. The two disciples are to follow a man carrying a water jar, presumably pretty obvious because back then that was woman’s work, and they are to ask him a loaded, carefully-phrased question about a guest room for a location of the Passover. This all goes according to plan, and Jesus and a large group of friends meet to eat in secret. Then he does the most appalling thing. Dresses down as a gentile slave and washes the excrement off their feet. Normally in the meal a slave would wash their hands, Jesus goes further. Much further.

If they forget his teaching about being servants to the world, they'll never forget this. It’s so startling, so shocking, so counter-cultural. You couldn't make it up. In fact, so much about this story you would never make up. If you wanted a tale about a powerful messiah who can change the whole of life, you wouldn't tell it this way – chock full of mistakes and misdemeanours. Cowardly good guys and a criminal's death.

Personally I love the part where Jesus predicts Peter's upcoming failure – he'll chop off the wrong ear, hook up with Judas to break into the high priest's house, and then spectacularly fall apart in public. Peter's heading for a breakdown and Jesus knows it. He tells him in front of everyone else. But he tells him something else too. Jesus predicts that after Peter's fallen apart, after the Rock has hit rock bottom, he will pick himself up again and then he must help his friends. Jesus can see beyond the catastrophe. He has already got his eyes on the next part of the plan for Peter. I love that. And I have hope because of that. When I crash and burn yet again, when you crash and burn yet again, Jesus can see beyond it, he's already got his eyes on plan B.

The New Genesis

For nine years I was responsible for retelling the events of Easter Sunday morning using live drama at the Lee Abbey holiday and conference centre, in Devon; and in doing so I discovered a big problem. Everyone knows what's going to happen.

It seems to me that Easter Sunday should make us smile, feel good and most importantly – give us a shock. But when you're revisiting a story from almost 2000 years ago that most people know – how can you put a twist in the tale? So each year I worked hard to put the unexpected back into the story, with events unravelling and characters appearing in ways the audience did not always see coming. That's what you get in the gospels, after all.

When the first Easter Sunday dawned, the disciples felt like death warmed up –- which of course is what Easter Sunday is partly about. They most likely had had little sleep and were still trying to work out how to avoid being arrested and punished for knowing Yeshua ben Yehosef. a.k.a. Jesus son of Joseph. When you read the four gospel accounts of what happened one thing is clear – there was confusion and chaos, with people running back and forth to the tomb. Think of what it's like when you lose your car keys and you're in a rush, how you search high and low, checking and rechecking places to find it. Or the lost passport, when you're desperate to get to the airport before your plane leaves. That's a glimpse of the madness of that morning. So, in the enactments we used to do, we threw in white-faced, mud clogged corpses wandering out of the undergrowth, (the resurrected bodies of those who had revived when Jesus died); Pontius Pilate sticking his head out of an upstairs window to tell everyone not to bother; Peter and John shoving their way through the audience, jostling to get there first; and most effective of all, a disguised Jesus who looked like the narrator of the story, and whose identity was only revealed right at the end when Mary threw him a stunned look of recognition and called out his name. The audience had spent half an hour with Jesus and had not realised it. The remembrance of that moment still gives me goose-bumps now. I loved it. It was the highlight of my Easter every year.

When Jesus walked out of that tomb on that extraordinary Sunday he may have been disappointed that there was no *Welcome back from the dead* party with streamers and champagne. Where was everybody? He'd told them he was coming after all! But it was an untidy day. Not at all carefully choreographed, and unlike most of the movie portrayals, was not reverent and sedate but full of misunderstandings and breathless encounters. I'm still waiting for the movie that really captures the life of that resurrection morning.

I particularly like one of the theories surrounding the Turin Shroud, and how the image came to be on that cloth. Some scientists believe there was a massive surge of energy in the body – a sort of new big bang -- and it was this that imprinted the image. Tom Wright describes Jesus's resurrection as the new Genesis, creation begun again. And the new Exodus too, the new journey out of captivity towards the Promised Land. However you see it – the gospels are four accounts coming at the story from different camera angles. I doubt if reading them again will give you any great shocks, but there may be one or two moments of surprise. What I hope above all is that these accounts make you feel better, not worse. Nothing, after all, can compare with the feelgood ending to feelgood end them all.

Getting Stoned

Ever think you know something then find you don't?

I have read and re-read and researched the story of the prodigal son for years, I have retold and revisited it in movies, shows, books, sermons and blogs. And just the other day a good friend of mine told me something I'd never heard before.

When the prodigal son returns home after running away, dumping his family and wasting all the money he had taken from his dad, his father does a shocking thing. He runs to meet him. Why? Because he has to run – to stop the villagers from stoning his son. I know – I'd never come across that before either.

You see, in the law of Moses, in Deuteronomy, a.k.a. Moses 5, in chapter 21, beginning at verse 18, it says that if a man has a stubborn, rebellious son who will not obey his parents, even though they discipline him, the father and mother must take the son before the leaders of the town. The parents must come clean about the son, using words like worthless and drunkard, if necessary. Then all the men of the town must get together and do something *really* spiritual. They must stone him to death. (I'm joking about the really spiritual bit, it's not in the original text.) Having done this they will have solved the problem and 'all Israel will hear about it and be afraid'.

A while ago a friend told me what a friend of his had jokingly said, when asked what he would do once his teenage daughter started bringing home boyfriends. 'I thought I'd shoot the first and then word would get round.' That's the principle in action here. Dispose of the first rebel and all the other lads will fall in line.

So here's a story of a rebellious son, who acts as if his father is dead. Takes his inheritance money and runs. He asks for his share of 'the property' not his share of 'the inheritance', as that came with responsibilities. He just wants hard cash. So the members of the local community would have declared that son to be dead. Gone forever. Shuffled off the mortal coil. Pushing up the daisies. What he had done was shameful, appalling, highly insulting. Everyone would have known about this boy and everyone would have agreed with this final 'cutting off' of him from his family and village. They would have acted as if he was dead. And if he ever came back they would have picked up the nearest fistful of rocks and made dead sure of the job.

What is so shocking is that the father refuses to act as if the boy is dead. He looks out for him, waits for him, longs for him to come back. He won't give up, won't act like everyone else. It's a tale of perseverance, undying hope against the odds and against the culture. Even against (sharp intake of breath) the law of Moses! The father refuses to believe it's all over and when he catches sight of the boy, he refuses to let him be attacked by the village. His running is in itself counter-cultural, respected men did not act that way, but he runs because it's more important to save his son. This is what makes his final words so powerful – 'my son was dead but is alive again.' Everyone else had declared the boy to be dead – but here's the father saying new life, resurrection has happened. His boy has returned from the dead.

The father wraps himself around his son, and if anyone chooses to throw a rock, it'll hit the father, not the son. Just like Jesus, taking the punishment on a Roman cross.

Back to Life

The Olympic Flame came to Lynton in 2012, and passed right outside our house! It was quite an occasion. Bunting everywhere, people in the streets, bomb disposal vans. And *that* torch, carrying the flame, which was passed on twice. Once outside our house and then later outside the church.

It struck me that it wasn't a bad little parable about the light of the world and the way people are drawn towards it. I mean, if a flame was ever global, it was that one. It did, after all, represent the nations. The crowds that gathered in Lynton, and I guess everywhere the Olympic Flame went, were a little reminiscent of another festival day – Palm Sunday. The light of the world comes to town and people flock to see him, decorate the streets, cheer and forget their day-to-day worries for a while.

Pentecost means fiftieth day – the fiftieth day after Passover. Both Jewish celebrations have rich meaning for Christians now. Passover has become Easter, Pentecost the birthday of the church – the day when we remember God's spirit hitting earth big time. Thousands begin to follow Jesus and – oh oh – they're all stuck with each other! You can choose your friends but you're stuck with the family of God.

My favourite Pentecost Bible reading is Ezekiel 37 – The Valley of Death. Ezekiel finds himself in a scene that wouldn't be out of place in a movie like *The Mummy*. Bits of skeletons litter the place and, as a priest, poor old Ezekiel really shouldn't have been immersing himself in so much dead stuff. But as ever, God took him to an 'unclean' place so he could show him something. The process of death and decay is reversed before his eyes, the bones rattle, re-form, get new muscles and skin, and (yikes) start walking around again!

One of the main results from the first day of Pentecost was people coming back to life. Developing a new sense of purpose and community. People caring for each other, sharing money and food. One of the great heroes of that time was a guy called Barnabas who sold his field and gave the money away. The day of Pentecost seemed to engender that kind of culture. The first Christian martyr, Stephen, was a guy whose job was looking after the poor and feeding the hungry.

On the day the flame came to town I started to hear news stories about how people were selling their torches online. And then I heard about the girl who had sold hers for something like £150,000 – so she could give the money to a charity which helped depressed people because her brother had taken his own life.

Ezekiel's picture of the dead coming back to life sums up the work of Jesus in our lives and communities. When Jesus was asked one day if he was really the Messiah he said, 'Look around you, the blind see, the lame walk, the lepers are cured, the deaf hear, the dead are raised to life, and the Good News is being preached to the poor.' People were coming back to life. Now, I'm a spiritual hobbit. I can't do those extraordinary things, I have to be honest about that. But I am inspired by the small things people do, the caring acts of kindness that change the world a little bit. Those tiny resurrection moments, which are not tiny to the God who appreciates every small detail.

Whilst working at the Lee Abbey Community in Devon I met a lady who worked in a school. She told me about the pupil who thanked her at the end of term for all she'd done. This lady could not really remember doing anything for this particular girl. But the girl replied, 'You always smiled at me.'

Kings and Queens

We are big *Horrible Histories* fans in our house. My older daughter has watched the BBC series repeatedly, so much so that she knows many of the songs, word for word. Because she loves them. And that is testimony to something I believe in – entertainment can be very informative. Before watching *Horrible Histories* my daughter knew nothing about history and was not interested. Now she knows more than I do. The *Rotten Rulers* song lists all the kings and queens of England, and many a youngster has learned the list by knowing the song. Entertaining tales stay with us, and more than that, we love to pass them on to others.

In one episode the creators imagined what it might be like if the first four King Georges formed a boy band and sang about their exploits whilst on the throne. Entertaining stuff it is too. According to the song, they were fairly self-indulgent and not popular with their people. Google Horrible Histories 4 King Georges and you might well find the song in question.

The reason I mention it now is that the song seems to me to represent the total opposite of the kind of king that Jesus is. When he walked the backstreets of Galilee he didn't look like a king at all. If you recall the Royal Wedding of Will and Kate a few years ago, it was an incredible occasion, a fantastic celebration. But it was of course chock full of pomp and regality. Servants and soldiers and the great and the good assembled, as well as the ordinary multitudes lining the streets. When Jesus visited places there was no such pomp and ceremony. He took royalty and made it accessible to all, often to the underprivileged and despised in society. He redefined being a king, or a prime minister, or a president. He himself tells a story about that. Here's my version:

It was uplifting news when Prince William and Kate Middleton decided enough was enough -- it was time to get hitched. It was time to get very publicly married. They set the date, mid-spring, when hopefully the weather would be good. They told the press, and put out countless interviews and photos. The country was going through a bad time so, all being well, this would lift everyone's spirits. The crowds would line the streets, the world would turn out, and billions would watch at home on their TV sets. This was going to be big.

Westminster Abbey was booked, invitations were sent out, the dressmakers got busy and all holiday was cancelled for the bodyguards. The day drew nearer and the forecast was... okay. But nothing could stop it now, the wheels were turning and soon the scene would be set for the wedding of the future king.

The day dawned. The soldiers had polished and pressed their uniforms, the caterers had been busy since before dawn, the horses were groomed to perfection. Kate's dress was a work of art and Will's uniform was... okay. Time for the kickoff.

But as William and his brother Harry set out for the Abbey the streets were strangely deserted. Tumbleweed drifted past the car. There was no one camping out. No visitors from far flung countries. The people hadn't yet turned out. In the Abbey there were spare seats, only half the choir turned up and they were clearly out of tune. The Archbishop was there and the Queen managed to roll up, but other important dignitaries were missing. Kate appeared and floated down the aisle in her perfect dress and William turned to her.

'You look beautiful,' he said, and she gave him a warm, confident smile. The marriage went ahead and they made their vows.

After the service they climbed aboard the royal carriage. And no one cheered. Because no one had come. No one cared.

As they rode back along the streets William and Kate caught sight of the families and individuals huddled around their televisions, watching Soap Operas and Reality TV, programmes like Cookery on Ice and Strictly Paint Drying.

One or two children ran out of front doors to watch the spectacle and William and Kate did their best to wave, but it was all so bewildering and confusing. Where was everyone? Why had they not come to the best event of the year? Didn't they want to see Kate's dress, didn't they want to witness a double kiss on the balcony? Apparently not.

Will leant over to Kate and whispered to her. No one heard, only Kate. But as soon as they arrived back at the palace a huge number of aides were sent out to invite those who slept on the streets all the time. Those who had not had the chance before to come to a royal wedding. The invitations went out and Kate and Will waited to see who would come.

A king throwing the doors of his palace wide, welcoming those who would choose to come, free of charge, citizens of a new kind of kingdom.

The Christmas Shop

Christmas Eve. A couple walk the aisles of a supermarket gathering up the food and frills for a cracking Christmas. Early on in their travels they spot the Christmas baby and scoop that into the trolley. Of course they must have the Christmas baby, what is Christmas about after all? Other things get added. Crackers, decorations, cake, mince pies, mulled wine, turkey, stuffing, sprouts (Really? You really want the sprouts? You know what they do to you…') Little by little the trolley fills up and it's clear there's going to be a problem. It's not big enough. They um and ah for a while, shift a few things around ('Don't squash the Yule Log!') and then the solution becomes clear. Put the baby to one side and pick it up later.

Of course. No problem. Why didn't we think of that earlier? Returning it to the shelf makes just enough room for one of those embarrassing Christmas jumpers, a large box of Quality Street and a few bits of extra tinsel. Perfect. On into the queue ('I don't think we'll risk the twelve items or less till, darling…') then it's wait, wait… ('We're going to miss the repeat of the 1974 Morecambe and Wise Christmas Show…') then a jolly festive chat to the check-out woman in the flashing Santa hat, load up the bags, wheel them to the car in the trolley and off. Christmas sorted.

Meanwhile, at the end of the day the shelves are cleared. Some of the stock is passed on to the food banks. Other bits are just placed out back with the bins. And later that night, as Christmas Eve is dying under the glimmering stars and the sound of parties and tellies echoes from street to street, a couple of folks of indeterminate age wander past the supermarket skips and hear a noise. They stop and come closer. There it is. The Christmas baby. They scoop it up, pull off one of their coats though the night is cold, and wrap it around the tiny child. They scuttle to an all-night drop-in, where a few prostitutes and homeless folks are getting festive soup and coffee. There they nurse the child and tell the story of the Christmas baby. And the few stragglers kneel, coo and wonder.

Cool to be Kind

This last half term week I have been speaking at Scargill House, in Yorkshire. A beautiful place. I sometimes draw on the favourite films of those attending the sessions, and as a result of doing that this week I discovered *Happy Go Lucky* directed by Mike Leigh. It's a movie about Poppy who is irrepressibly optimistic and upbeat, to the point of embarrassment sometimes.

There are many movies about the foolish person who unmasks 'the wise'. Think of Tom Hanks as Forrest Gump or Charlie Chaplin as the hapless Tramp. Fools who show up ‘the wise’. Fyodor Dostoevsky used this device in his novel *The Idiot*. No one wants to look foolish of course and society these days puts so much emphasis on being cool, looking right, appearing the way the adverts tell us we should, even though we know the ads are edited and airbrushed.

Shane Claiborne, author of *The Irresistible Revolution,* tells about a time when he visited a school and was introduced as 'the coolest Christian on the planet'. At the time he had his hair in dreadlocks, so, on hearing this introduction, he walked on and asked for a pair of scissors. When he was given some he cut off his dreadlocks in front of the pupils and told them that being a Christian is not about being cool, but about following Jesus. Of course, the pupils all then thought him cool for doing this!

How much of an idiot did Jesus look when he let a 'fallen woman' (nowadays we might describe her as a bit of a ‘trainwreck’) bust into his space, publicly wash his feet and then let down her hair to dry them. An act so revealing and intimate in his day that it was toe-curlingly embarrassing for the other men sitting near him. She, like so many of those who met Jesus, acted inappropriately. But he wasn't bothered about the right behaviour. He was never bothered about looking good or cool. To Jesus acting cool meant acting kindly. You can read about Jesus and this 'trainwreck' in Luke's gospel blog, chapter 7 from verse 36.

I guess it's certainly possible to be a Christian and look cool. But Jesus and the prophets show us that we need to be prepared to shove coolness in the dustbin at times, when acting compassionately is more important. When bringing kindness to others means looking a bit of an idiot. When Jesus watched a load of rich, cool guys putting their fistfuls of money into the offering box, he sided with a poor old lady who had hardly anything to give away. She quickly placed her 10p coin in the slot and scurried off, and Jesus pointed her out so that she has gone down in history. Who knows what the other folks gave. I mean that, who knows? We don't, because no one else went down in history for their gift that day. Just the poor humble widow, who has become a model for us all.

Sitcom Bombs

When scribblers sit down to write situation comedies or gripping, edge-of-the-seat dramas they make sure of one thing. They plant a lot of 'bombs'. These are events early in the story which later on will prove effective, funny, or plot-twisting. For example in an episode of the sitcom *Dad's Army* Sergeant Wilson is asked to prime a box of grenades, but being of a sensitive nature he primes them with dummy explosives. Later in the story Captain Mainwaring finds himself with a grenade down the back of his trousers. Will it go off? Will he be ex-Captain Mainwaring? Will his bottom be no more? Not at all, because that 'Sergeant Wilson decision' earlier on means that when the pin is pulled... absolutely nothing will happen. The intention of course is that we will forget the earlier incident and be surprised when that particular bomb eventually does, or in this case doesn't, go off.

It may seem a slightly convoluted idea, but I think that following Jesus means we sometimes plant bombs like this. Doing things which will later bear good fruit. We most likely won't see the effect when the bomb eventually does go off, but that shouldn't stop us planting a few of these things. To put it in farming terms, we sow seeds and trust they will grow. Jesus once said that the farmer works hard, sows his crop, goes to sleep, gets up again, goes back to sleep, gets up again, goes back to... I think you know where this is going. The farmer continues with his daily routine, and all the while the seed is growing. He doesn't necessarily understand how the seed is growing, but that does not stop it. I post videos on YouTube, and whether or not I check them every day the number of people viewing them gradually goes up. I do nothing more to them, I carry on with other things. I go to bed, I get up, I go to bed, I get up, I go to bed... etc. And all the time the number of views on YouTube grows. It's as if it has a life of its own. (Mark chapter 4 verses 26-28.)

So we plant seeds, we lay those bombs of kindness, truth, justice and good news, and then we leave them to do their work. Very occasionally we may just get to see the results, or some of the results anyway. I recently heard someone describe how, years after slogging away at a kids' club on an estate, they had bumped into one of the boys who had attended the club. He had been through some very difficult years, but had not forgotten the seeds planted in the kids' club. Now he had become a dedicated Christian, working with an organisation to spread the good news of Jesus. The bomb had been planted, and at the right time, boom! It had brought new life into that young man's life.

'Never tire of planting benign bombs,' said St Paul to the Galatians, 'for in good time they will go boom! And good things will come of it.' He didn't quite put it like that, but that's what the old saint meant. (You can read it for yourself in Galatians chapter 6 verse 9.)

Jesus Was Indie

I have been watching a documentary on BBC4 called *Music for Misfits*, it's about the beginning and rise of Indie (or independent) music and record labels. It all began in the anarchic days of punk when a band called the Buzzcocks decided to record and press their own single without the aid of a record company. The result was a four track EP called *Spiral Scratch*. It may sound incredible now but no one had really considered doing this before. Bands went to major record labels and asked for a recording contract. If the major label thought they were good and would make money then they signed them up. Doing it the Buzzcocks way meant that you didn't have to create the kind of music that pleased the big money men. You could be true to the music you believed in. Others have since followed in their wake, and many independent labels have come and gone, championing new music and sometimes paving the way for new forms of rock and pop music. Lecture over.

The reason I mention this is that when I was enthusing to my wife about the *Spiral Scratch* tale she happened to say, 'Jesus was indie.' At which point my eyes lit up and I nodded feverishly. Of course he was indie. Why hadn't I thought of that? Jesus was operating in a totally different way, not relying upon the established systems of his day, on the big companies and the money men. Instead he operated on the margins, and connected with others who were on the margins too. When he did bump into the 'majors' of his day it often resulted in conflict. He wasn't interested in their games and deals. His was a different tune, a different kind of music.

There have been times when the major record companies have taken note of the indies and come looking to sign a few of their bands. But the outcome has not always been happy. Once an exciting new band has been wooed into the corridors of success the majors bring in their own slick producers, and what was once a new, edgy, groundbreaking sound is tamed and tutored into something else. Something acceptable, something mainstream.

Jesus has never really been mainstream, though the church has often aligned itself with the establishment. The reality is that his way of life is edgy, disruptive, not always easy on the ears. Hating the world, carrying a bloody Roman cross, and telling culture-bucking stories will get you into trouble. The majors may have offered Jesus a deal, but he could never water down his sound. He had faced that temptation in the desert and had clarified his position back then. He had come to reach those rejected by the mainstream, those who were hungry for righteousness and justice, rather than sales and success.

So I reckon my wife is right.
Jesus is indie.
Always has been always will be.

Limitless?

I have just finished watching a movie called *Limitless*, an intelligent action thriller starring Bradley Cooper and Robert DeNiro, about a guy who discovers a drug which enables him to access 100% of his brain. The word on the street is that we only use 20% of the brain, (although this is really just an urban myth), but NZT48 enables anyone who takes it to access all of it. Learning, perceiving, remembering, formulating and reacting all become dramatically heightened.

When struggling writer Eddie Morra takes the NZT drug he finishes his book in four days, learns to play the piano instantly and masters speaking a fistful of languages. He can see things much more clearly, and see himself and his surroundings with incredible clarity. He can think and plan much more effectively and astutely.

Eddie not only completes his novel but, enabled by this new heightened intelligence, embarks on a whole new existence. It takes him from zero to hero overnight. And his new found brilliance makes him an awful lot of money. When he starts displaying side effects though, he realises he is in dangerous waters and suddenly there is talk of coming off the drug. Oops, now he has a problem.

I guess we'd all like to be more successful, to cut out our blundering moments, our mistakes and embarrassments. It would be great if learning new things could be done overnight, and we could be much more self-aware so we are always in control of our surroundings. But life really isn't like that. And not even for Eddie Morra. As he becomes much more successful he attracts unwanted attention and eventually ends up with two bodyguards, living in a high-security apartment. Life is fraught with difficulty and no matter what we do, sooner or later it seems to ambush us. Which reminds me of what Jesus said one day, 'In this world you'll have some trouble.' He knew all about that of course because he had plenty of it.

It's easy to imagine Jesus as some kind of limitless superman, floating above everything, never having to put up with the problems of normality. But that isn't the picture we get in the Bible. Instead he often found himself engaged in arguments and slanging matches. People misjudged and insulted him. His friends and family tried to micro-manage him at times, and his enemies threatened to take his life.

However, the film did make me wonder whether he had one or two *Limitless* moments. Times when he saw himself and the world with heightened clarity, times when he spotted very clearly what needed to be done. His long hours on a Roman cross might have been like that, as he viewed the realities of a world in pain, a damaged global history strewn with desperate people and lonely lives. And the requirements needed for solving that epic problem. Perhaps too when he met people haunted by their failures and their past and their demons, he saw them in a way no one else could. Saw their potential and their value. When he met those who were self-righteous and full of their own importance, he saw their potential too, saw through their well-constructed fronts and their kingdom building.

But ultimately the whole point of Jesus was not to be a superman, but to be someone we could relate to. The ultimate creator who diminished himself and came to walk in our frail shoes, treading the paths of us plodding, unique people. God discovering what it is like to be human. So I don't think Jesus was anything like a guy on NZT48. He was a man with his feet firmly on planet earth.

Questions

I was reading about Katy Perry a while ago and I discovered a couple of things which set me thinking. Katy Perry, at that time, was one of the biggest stars in the world, having had five number one songs in the US. She was, as they say, hot. But she took a long time to get going, dumped by four record companies along the way. Success did not come overnight. It took a lot of sweat and perseverance. I'm often encouraged by stories of those who don't give up. The actor Mark Ruffalo attended 600 auditions before getting an acting break. 600!! 600???!!!!! Easy to type those little numbers, isn't it? 600. There I did it again. How long does it take to attend 600 auditions?

The other thing I noticed though was that Katy Perry comes from an evangelical Christian family, and she made the comment that while growing up she wasn't encouraged to question things. Those of us inside the Christian faith often feel we must defend it to the point of excluding all kinds of other viewpoints. Which is odd because it wasn't Jesus's approach at all. He was a rabbi and as such encouraged debate and argument and the 'what do you think about this' kind of approach. The main form of teaching was by telling stories, and once a story was out there anyone could comment and wrestle with its meaning. Personally I think more opportunity to ask questions in a sermon might not be a bad thing.

So – please let's not be afraid to search and question. There's a great little verse in the biblical book of Proverbs chapter 25 verse 2. 'It is God's job to hide things, ours to search them out.' If we don't dig around, question, search out – we may miss something vital.

Evan 'elp Us!

Just read that Mr Jim *Bruce Almighty* Carrey is considering making a follow up to his 2003 big money-spinning movie. My first thought of course was there has already been a 'sequel' – *Evan Almighty*, which thrust Bruce's much-maligned work colleague, Evan Baxter, into the limelight. On first release this film was itself much-maligned, being much more an environmentally-catastrophic family comedy than *Bruce Almighty* was. I've seen *Evan Almighty* a lot, my daughter loves it, and the more I have watched it the more thought-provoking I have found it to be. For one thing it shows how blooming embarrassing it can be to try and follow the calling of God. The Old Testament prophets were tough guys, with tough jobs. And at times, like Evan, they must have looked like idiots. But as it says in the writings of one such prophet, Jeremiah, (don't invite him to one of your feelgood parties, he'll bring the temperature right down) 'Best not to glory in riches or strength or wisdom (or celebrity or fame) instead glory in this -- that you know and understand the God who loves kindness, justice and doing what is right.'

I heard on the radio the other day that we can now expect more floods and water shortages in the future. Call me old-fashioned but there's surely something that doesn't quite add up there, but – hey! – what do I know? You don't have to go far in the Bible to find there's nothing new under the sun. In Genesis chapter 6 we have Noah's flood and by Genesis chapter 12 we have Abraham on the run from a famine in the desert. Disasters and catastrophe are littered like news bulletins throughout the good book.

Evan Almighty is of course a new take on the Noah story, and as such you have to wonder about the massive boat and the exotic animals when it's a localised flooding issue. But that's where successive viewings have made me think again. The movie is not about the animals at all. The ark and the creatures are just there to get the people's attention. Evan builds a boat so people will stop and wonder. And ultimately change direction. Very much in the tradition of the Old Testament guys. They did plenty of unnecessary things to jam a stick in the spokes of everyday life, to stop people in their tracks, to wake them up. Ezekiel burnt crap, built models, dug holes in walls, refused to speak and did some excessive haircutting. Jeremiah buried his underwear and Isaiah didn't bother wearing any at all. Just went down the shops butt-naked for a while. All of this was to wake people up to the God who loves kindness, justice and doing what is right. They may have appeared weird, but they did what they did to cause a Godly fuss.

Tom Shadyac, the director of *Bruce* and *Evan* said that his first film, *Bruce Almighty,* explored what happens to a person when they are given extraordinary power. The second, *Evan*, explores what happens when they have their power taken away. Evan becomes a prophet and gets weaker. He loses his wealth, respect, cool and back garden to the biggest boat in movie history. A few years ago a Lynx advert came along, looking a lot like a scene from *Evan Almighty*, using similar boat imagery. Hordes of women flocked to a particularly good-looking, and sweet-smelling Noah, desperate for the cabin next door to him on his big boat. The advert tapped into our ongoing fears that it will all end badly, and suggested we make sure that we smell right when it does.

When Rome fell to the barbarian hordes the locals thought it was the end of the world. How could Rome fall? Impossible. They thought that the end of everything was at hand and believed that the mouths of volcanoes would open up and swallow all the grievous sinners. That was 1500 years ago, and so far, life still goes on. I can't help thinking that there is something in our DNA, some hardwiring that makes us feel one day this world as it is will change or come to an end. That there is something temporary about this life. The moviemakers love exploring this – films like *2012, Armageddon, The Day After Tomorrow, The Road, The Book of Eli* and *Seeking a Friend for the End of the World* have all been to the end of days and back. They all tell tall tales about the impending final moments of earthdom.

The ultimate message of the biblical Book of Revelation is to hang on, keep believing and not give in to worldly pressures. Whatever may happen to this crazy little place called earth. One day Jesus will usher in a new reality, a kingdom of justice, peace and endless hope. Till then, 'Don't be worried and upset, believe in God,' said Jesus, 'and believe in me.'
John recorded it in his gospel blog, chapter 14, verse 1.

Are We Nearly There Yet?

Just hearing on the radio about a family starting their journey to their summer holiday with the message, 'There's 9 hours to go...' made me think about the way we're always desperate to be there. As kids yes, but as adults too. There's an old saying about how the journey is more important than the destination. But suppose there *is* only the journey? Suppose you're heading somewhere you know you'll never reach? Would you still travel? Imagine a lifetime of the kids in the back saying, 'Are we nearly there yet?' in that sing-song voice.

You could say that's life. Because in many ways – it is. A while back I read an interview with Andrew Garfield, who became the *Amazing Spiderman* for two films. In the article the young British actor said that it was a lifelong dream to play the web-spinning guy, but on doing it he was disappointed, because it felt like just another job. Often the waiting is the best part. Most of us feel like we're heading somewhere, but we haven't arrived. And if we do achieve one dream, it seems to be replaced by another. We slog up one peak only to see the next one come into view. We never truly arrive, and maybe that's because we're designed to be travellers more than settlers.

The Bible is full of travellers who never quite finish their journeys. They are very aware that they are travellers, they don't feel at home here. They are a bunch of sore thumbs. Abraham and his wife Sarah began a trek they would never finish. Their lives were stagnating and they felt God call them into the unknown. So they left everything, their way of life, their extended family, the familiarity of their home and village, and they went. And they spent the rest of their lives on the move. It was a journey fraught with the unexpected. They encountered famine, danger, fear and annihilation. And God. Who never left them.

The writer of the book of Hebrews is unknown but we're fairly sure it wasn't Enid Blyton, Jeffrey Archer, Agatha Christie, J K Rowling or Roald Dahl. What we do know is that he included, in chapter 11, a list of those who followed God, but did not reach their destination in this life. In verse 13 he says, 'All these faithful ones died without receiving what God had promised them, but they saw it all from a distance and welcomed the promises of God. They agreed that they were no more than foreigners and nomads here on earth.'

Foreigners and nomads. An apt description for you and I too. On that journey, forever asking if we're there yet, and like those faithful ones, only glimpsing the prize from a distance.

So if you feel ill-at-ease with life, you're not alone. If you feel you haven't arrived, if your dreams are elusive, or you have realised them and found them wanting, it could all be a sign that you are simply still travelling. Still tracing that path that will one day lead somewhere amazing, somewhere *other*. Once the unexpected wonders, surprises, depressions and struggles of this life are done.

Just Like the Spanish Inquisition

It was an incredible, sensory-overloading extravaganza. Fireworks, drummers, smoking chimneys and the Olympic flame hoisted in the air on 204 blazing petals. Not to mention Beckham, Bean and Bond all jostling to steal the show. I was just sorry the Queen didn't greet 007 with the words, 'I've been expecting you, Mr Bond.'

Danny Boyle's culturally-laden opening ceremony for the 2012 Olympics was hailed as breathtaking and bonkers, unpredictable and inventive. Danny Boyle himself said he hoped it was charming, not annoying. It seemed to me this was a ceremony devised by a visual storyteller. Three hours jammed with tales and images, a million references hurled at the world through sound, movement, music and movies. My guess is no one got them all. And if you are not that familiar with Britain's past much of it may have been baffling. Hopefully most people have come across Messrs Bean and Bond. One thing's for sure, like the Spanish Inquisition, no one could have expected it. (Another cultural reference there!)

The Bible is of course jammed with the same kind of visual storytelling. Unfortunately we can't watch it as we did with Danny Boyle's vision. We only have the words on the page. There are hundreds of songs with no tunes. (Would they be like Arctic Monkeys, Shirley Bassey, Frank Sinatra, Paul McCartney or Emeli Sandé?) There are stories full of cultural humour and local references that we don't get. And big screen, surround sound displays without the big screens or the surround sound. Try and talk someone through Danny Boyle's extravaganza at the bus stop today and you won't even come close. They'll most likely be drifting off before you've even got through the first twenty minutes. I only watched it on TV so I didn't get the full experience at all – what must it have been like to have been there, receiving it all live, or dancing and acting and drumming as part of it all?

So when we read books like Revelation we must keep in mind that we only have words on a page. The author John was there, at that sensory-overloading, big screen, surround sound experience. He saw things that were shocking, quirky, mind-bending, eye-popping and ear-bleeding. Thunderous voices, killer locusts, blazing lamps, emerald rainbows, explosions in the sky, a cast of millions. Danny Boyle would have been proud. No wonder this book, mysteriously labelled Revelation, is the hardest to get, the most difficult to Reveal, it's like reading a long list of what happened in the Olympic Stadium on the night of 27th July 2012. 'Then Team Kuwait came in, then Team Kyrgyzstan, then Team Lao People's Democratic Republic... it was so awesome.' As the saying goes, 'You should have been there.'

The Bible is jammed with this kind of visual storytelling. Until we get a 3D, smelli-visual, all-singing, all-dancing, all-drumming Good Book we'll have to settle for a 2D version.

The Bible. Bring your imagination.

Limping Home

I find confession a strange, muddling, confusing experience. I often wonder if I have confessed enough, used the right words, felt sorry enough.

When it comes to bringing my misdemeanours to God, I wonder if, like the prodigal, I will always come back home looking to strike a deal, to earn my forgiveness, to be a hired worker. Because the opposite is so hard to comprehend. This thing called agape – this gift of forgiveness and welcome, this free offer of love and embrace, that we cannot earn. It's hard to get it into one's being. It's not that I have not experienced these things, I have, but you and I live in a world where love is conditional. And so it is these conditional examples and reminders about the nature of love that frequently come to us.

I believe absolutely in the good gifts of God. I believe in the mysterious sacrifice of Jesus, the death that brought a new start for us all. But I often struggle to *feel* it. It's almost easier if I just get on and live with that gift woven through my life, not examining it, or checking that I've really received it. Once someone asks me to make a study of it then I'm in trouble. Then I start having doubts as to how forgiven I really am, if I really have said sorry for everything and covered all the bases.

The obvious deal to lay on the table is the promise to 'never do that again' and so earn this slate-wiping. But I've been trying that for years and I'm old enough to know that these are very often empty promises. A few years ago I had a kind of picture in my mind whilst praying. It was of myself, covered in all kinds of disgusting muck, kneeling at the foot of the cross and clinging onto it for dear life. And it seemed as if God was saying to me something like – it doesn't matter whether or not you feel clean. You may always struggle to feel it, but at the cross it's okay, you are forgiven. That's the way it is.

I've mentioned this before but in this context I'll mention it again. When the prodigal came limping home he had all the wrong credentials. His story is based on that of Jacob, back in Genesis. Jake came home rich, successful and married with lots of children. In that culture that was seen as a sign of God's blessing. He had all the right credentials. The prodigal comes home having been a failure, a loser who has no wives or children, he has just been sleeping with prostitutes. Paying for a futile kind of satisfaction. He has all the wrong credentials. Yet, the father runs and welcomes him. God is, shockingly, on his side.

So I think I will always struggle with this desire to feel free, and also with the guilt that can then pile on top of my inability to feel forgiven and free. And when I make yet another limping pilgrimage home, looking to strike another deal with the father, he will have to remind me yet again, that he doesn't do deals. But one of the great things I also believe is that God understands. He knows what I'm like, he wired me up, he knows what all humans are like. He became one. And Hebrews chapter 4 verse 15 assures us that Jesus, our High Priest, understands our weaknesses. So feeling the right things, and correctly perceiving God's forgiveness becomes less of an issue. I'll never comprehend it, best just to trust with what little faith I have, and keep putting one foot in front of the other. It's limping home that matters.

God knows. God cares.

A Bit of Shopping or a Gold Medal?

We discovered something amazing yesterday. My wife Lynn used to be taken to playgroup by an Olympic athlete! Her name was Ann Packer, and in 1964 she and her fiancée Robbie Brightwell went to Tokyo. Not for a holiday, but to compete in the Olympics. I knew her name well but didn't know why, so we looked her up and found her story to be remarkable. She went to the Games in '64, hoping to win gold in the 400 metres final, but was beaten into second place by Australian Betty Cuthbert. A few days later she planned to go on a shopping trip with some friends. However, her fiancé persuaded her to reconsider her plans. And instead of going shopping she decided to enter the 800 metres – a race she had only ever run seven times before. So she entered and made it through the heats. However, she got into the final as the slowest qualifier.

At 400 metres she was sixth in the race, by 600 metres she was third, and in the last 200 metres her sprint finish kicked in and she outran them all, winning the gold against all the odds. Afterwards she said, 'I knew nothing about the event but being so naive was probably to my advantage; it meant I did not have any limitations in my head regarding what I should or could do. Ignorance proved to be bliss.'

It would be another 40 years before another British woman would win gold in the 800m – when Kelly Holmes won both the 800m and 1500m finals in Athens. I love this story of Ann Packer, bucking the trend, and winning against all the odds. Her win has gone down in history as one of the greatest sporting achievements.

I so often limit myself, being cowed by life and peer pressure. Conforming to what is the norm, what is expected, what usually happens. We get fixed in our ways don't we? And breaking out is not at all easy. If Jesus had followed the usual, expected pattern he would have continued in his earthy father's work. Perhaps becoming a champion carpenter-builder. But he heard another call, a counter-cultural call, and he left behind one job for another. He encountered a lot more hostility in his new calling, but in doing what he did, he changed the world. It was costly for him, demanding, but he took the risk, stepped out and went against the norm.

50 Shelves of Mishmash

Just been wandering around WH Smiths in a daze, as I sometimes do. I love books but find the presence of so many in one place a little overwhelming. So I thought I'd check out the 'spiritual' books. Man, what a weird mixture. Everything from *The Karma Sutra* and *Sensational Sex* to Dannii Minogue's *My Style* and of course that classic *The Man Diet*. The biggest thing about the display was Gok Wan's face, who for some reason had two massive books there on how to dress better. I was heartened to see there were lots of Bibles and a couple of books by theologian Tom Wright plus, strangely, a guidebook to Rob Bell's *Love Wins*, without any sign of a copy of *Love Wins* anywhere on the shelves.

I couldn't help wondering how on earth anyone would find what they were looking for amongst this particular literary mishmash. In fact it's hard to imagine why anyone would wander up to that shelf – unless they were an overweight, sex-starved, badly dressed, lapsed Protestant who was confused about Rob Bell's book.

I wonder whether we Christian writers are losing the battle for hearts and minds. Are there no contemporary, entertaining, accessible reads out there communicating the faith to the blokes and blokettes on the street? Are we not able to speak the kind of language that the gospels first used? Street lingo. The good news for the readers of *The Sun* and *Fifty Shades of Grey*. Talking of which I also noticed in WH Smiths that the clones are out. Fifty books of grey mercilessly impersonating *Fifty Shades of Grey* have appeared. All with the same kind of monochrome cover, all cashing in on the way we've now discovered sex. Everything from *80 Shades of Magnolia* to *5000 Chunks of Dairy Milk*.

That seemed to be the gist of it anyway. I didn't want to be seen in public studying the titles too closely.

It's frustrating trying to communicate with the world at large about God. Christian publishers seem to want 'christian' books, with words like praying, evangelism and purpose-driven on the cover. And books like that won't often make it into Smiths alongside Dannii and Gok. And we Christians seem cautious about communicating in ways which don't seem very 'christian'. It's not easy to put yourself into the shoes of those who are outside of the faith, to see things from their perspective. But it seems to me that this is what's required. To move away from our christian clichés and phraseology and tell the story of the faith using ideas and images that people can easily grab hold of.

There's a song by Savage Garden called *I bet he was cool* and it has lines like this -- 'Every once in a while I shoot the breeze, I like to talk about Jesus Christ. If he passed you by would you be scared... would you believe in him? Would you bust your asses to get him institutionalized?' It references *Star Wars*, Tommy Hilfiger, Quentin Tarantino and Elvis. It uses humour and irony and asks questions. Just the kind of tools Jesus used. And it reminds me to talk about normal stuff when attempting to communicate about God.

There's so much negative spin these days concerning God and Jesus. People have been hurt by religion in the past and sometimes the very mention of certain names and words can light a raging fire that no man can put out. So using stories and other creative ways to speak of God can sometimes sidestep the negative baggage. I heard Adrian Plass use a good phrase about Jesus's gripping yarns. People in his day had all kinds of strange ideas about God so he told them parables – 'the story comes in the door, while the truth slips in through a side window'.

Film-makers often employ this kind of approach, making great entertainment that leaves us thinking and moved. Perhaps one day I'll get round to writing a book jammed full of biblical ripping tales that makes it into WH Smiths religious section, no doubt wedged between *The Karma Sutra* and *The Man Diet*...

Mountain Tops

Just been chatting with a friend about the good times we have and the experiences which give us a real shot in the arm. It might be climbing or surfing, knitting or catching up with friends, cooking or eating, watching a favourite team or film. It makes me think about Jesus taking his best mates up a mountain one day to get a genuine *mountain top* experience. Jesus is starting on the last leg of his marathon mission, the hardest part. So he takes time out to recharge and refocus and while doing so has an extraordinary, supernatural experience. The view from a mountain top is very different. His mates are blown away and, with his usual lack of tact and understanding, Peter suggests they stay up there forever, making some shelters so they can camp out.

But Jesus is having none of it – his whole attitude is simple. They have come up the mountain... so they can go back down again. His mates are confused, they are probably expecting this to be the end of the road – after all, nothing will top this extraordinary experience. 'Let's stay here forever soaking up the good times.' But they miss the point. When Jesus takes them back down they are immediately plunged into the thick of it again – people making demands on them, things going wrong, mishaps and misdemeanours crashing in on them like debris from a car wreck.

One of the things I love about Jesus is that he gets reality. He's rooted in it, faces up to it, understands how it works. When he comes down the mountain and is hit by a train of demands and emotions and catastrophes he kind of lets out a 'Uggghhhhhh!' type of sound. A heartfelt, guttural cry of frustration. I think we've all been there. You get back from holiday, or that encouraging time with friends, or that confidence-boosting conference and suddenly you find the roof has fallen in back home, the bills are piled up on the doormat and there's the great-grandmother of all leaks in the bathroom. Life happens. And you wonder where the peace and power and inspiration that you found in your time out have gone.

Jesus gets that. And it seems that the very reason he went up the mountain was because he knew that things were going to get extraordinarily hard very soon. He went away to steel himself, to recharge, to get perspective. And as wonderful as that time was – it wasn't an end in itself. It was just the start. It was recharging his batteries. It was so he could begin that last long lonely climb up towards a hill called Golgotha. It also opened the eyes of his friends and crystallised what they had begun to glimpse, that he was the Messiah.

So if your week ends with an anti-climax or a catastrophe of some sort – Jesus understands – he knows what it's like. He's been there. Done that. And let out the groan of frustration.

You can check out the full story in Matthew's biblical blog, chapter 17 verses 1to 23.

The Big Day

Today is our wedding anniversary. (It may well not be so on the day you read this of course, but at some point this year it will have come and gone.) Two decades of awesomeness. (Don't worry about cards – just send the cash.) The year we got married *Four Weddings and a Funeral* was playing everywhere. It was the smash hit movie. I'm afraid it wasn't *my* smash hit movie. Nothing to do with Hugh Grant, I have enjoyed a lot of his stuff. Call me old-fashioned but I just found it a little cynical towards that age-old institution I was about to enter. I know. I need to get a sense of humour. To be honest I don't tend to get on too well with most films that feature the word *Wedding* in the title. *Four Weddings, The Wedding Singer, The Wedding Planner, Muriel's Wedding, My Best Friend's...* you get the picture...

I'm afraid they all tend to pass me by like an overlong best man speech. Sorry. Probably my favourite film that features any wedding connection is *Kill Bill Volume 2*, in which Uma Thurman plays a character called The Bride. But it's not a romantic comedy. Not by any stretch of the imagination.

The church is often thought of as a bride, but that doesn't cut much ice with me either. You see, I can't picture myself in the dress, and as for throwing a bouquet... hmm. This image is often proclaimed joyfully in songs and sermons but it just doesn't do it for me. And I'm sure I'm not alone, there must be other guys out there who find themselves floundering with the idea of appearing in public in a big meringue outfit.

But there is hope. In the Old Testament book of Isaiah, written by... who was it again? Oh yea... Isaiah, you can find another wedding picture. A more inclusive one. In chapter 61 verse 10 the prophet says he's blown away by the presence of God, and the way that this has transformed his life. He says it's as if God has given him a new Armani suit (other tailors are available) and dressed him to the nines like a bridegroom. He feels that good. And if the bride image is the one that really appeals – well, he includes that one too. Saying it's like a bride all dressed up and dazzling with jewels. It's worth noting that these images are then followed with a line about justice. The arrival of God isn't just about making me feel better, it's about restoring full and healthy life to the earth. The universe even.

When he was walking around the backstreets of Galilee, hanging out with the oppressed and the pub crawlers, Jesus described himself as being like a bridegroom, inviting people to something which was full of life, colour, wine, food, promises, hope and partying. Now we all know weddings can go wrong, they can be teeming with old family feuds. But the do that Jesus has in mind is different. It's a place of welcome and good times. Anyone can come, just knock on the door.

Beating the System

In John's blog about his time with Jesus, in chapter 15, John records Jesus as saying something significant. 'You did not choose me, I chose you.'

This has led to many debates about the P word – predestination. How much free will do we have? I heard a good quote about that just this week. ‘If Jesus hadn't made his choices, we wouldn't be able to make ours.’ His choice to set aside the supreme quality of life with his father, in order to step into our shoes and ultimately submit himself to oppression, squalor and corruption on earth. His choice to live and die and live again. We can debate about the P word, and many other high concepts, but that may be missing the point. You see, when Jesus looked at those fishermen and collaborators and prostitutes and rebels, and spoke of choosing them, he was being quite literal. Just saying it like it was. And a strange thing it was too.

Jesus did choose them. He went out looking. He spotted them at work and chose them to come with him. They then made their choices. But they would never have come looking for him, would have had no choice to make if he had not come looking for them.

Jesus had no reputation as a rabbi. He had no training, nothing that would put him out there. No profile on Twitter or Facebook. No blog or poster campaign. If Jesus had waited for others to pick him he may well have been waiting a long time. Like those of us who were not good at sport at school and ended up stuck, sadly shivering on the touchline. The last to be chosen for the football team.

Usually rabbis got trained up from an early age, and then others would come and ask if they could be followers. The followers would choose the rabbi. The rabbi would not go wandering about looking for them. But not Jesus. He does it the wrong way. He goes looking for followers. And there may have been a very good reason for this. He wanted to bypass the system.

In the film *The Untouchables* good guys Sean Connery and Kevin Costner go looking for some reliable cops to help them crack corruption in Chicago. So they go to the training school, bypassing the cops who are already part of the system, because the system is tainted. Jesus does the same thing. He doesn't want those who already feel religious. Those caught up in a system that's bound up with the wrong code of practice. He wants others – those who aren't very spiritual. And know it. He wants to start afresh with apples straight from the tree, not fruit from the corrupted supply in the basket. It's worth noting that when Matthew wrote about his time with Jesus he specifically remembered that Jesus had said, 'Blessed are the poor in spirit.' In other words, those who aren't very holy. Matthew was himself a party-throwing tax collector, working for the hated Romans. It meant a lot to him that you didn't have to be a good person to follow Jesus. It means a lot to many of us.

It was a humble thing to do too. Jesus going out there, looking for friends. Not on a pedestal. Not in a stained glass window, or a big car. Jesus walking the streets, some of them quite mucky, keeping an eye out for those who are interested, those who may not feel very acceptable, but matter so much to him.

Wiser, Not Older

The other day we watched the film *Groundhog Day* again, this time with our daughter Amy. Afterwards we had a great discussion. Groundhog Day is about Phil, a cynical, selfish weatherman sent to Punxsutawney to report on the eponymous Groundhog Day. This is a day when a local furry critter will supposedly predict whether there will be an early spring or not. At the end of the day, as Phil and two colleagues head for home a blizzard sets in and they are forced to spend a second night in Punxsutawney. However, when Phil wakes up the next morning it is Groundhog Day all over again. And the next morning it is Groundhog Day yet again. Something strange has happened to time. He is caught.

Early in the movie, as Phil begins to realise he is trapped in the same day, he turns to a local guy and tells him of his predicament. Every day is the same, nothing changes. The local guy replies, 'Yep. Sounds about right.' And I suddenly realised, at the heart of this extreme film there is something quite normal – life can trap you. This is a story for all those who feel exactly like Phil, trapped in the same day, with no way out, making no progress. Nothing ever changes and we're going nowhere.

Phil's reaction to his predicament takes several turns. At first he tries being mad, bad and outrageous, punching people he can't stand, stealing money from a security firm, and learning as much as he can about the local hotties one day, so the next he can successfully chat them up and hustle them into bed. But after a while this lifestyle starts to unravel and despair overtakes him, so he tries to kill himself. Again, and again, and again. Without any success. Every morning he wakes up to the sound of Sonny and Cher singing *I got you Babe* at exactly the same time on the same radio show. Every day is still Groundhog Day and people are still heading to find out whether spring will come early.

This is a great piece of comedy that strikes at the very heart of what it is to be human. What will we do with the days we have? What will we make of our time? How will we treat others in our days? What are our priorities and where do we find meaning each 24 hours? I won't spoil it if you have not seen this film, but as you might expect, Phil is on a learning curve here. As we all are.

It seems to me that one of the many questions posed by this film is this – would you do good if it had no lasting consequence? Would you help that person today if you had to help them again tomorrow, and your helping them each day does not accumulate in any way? There are probably plenty of folks out there who do live that kind of life.

When we were chatting about the movie the other day we posed the question – which day would you live again and again? My daughter Amy said, 'Not a Sunday' and when I asked why she replied, 'Church!' When we considered the possibilities we decided any day would do, because there are no consequences to your actions. So you can skive school or work. You can go anywhere. As long as you can get there within 24 hours of course. I asked Amy if Phil was getting older with each passing Groundhog Day, and she said, 'No, just wiser!' which I liked.
I hope you get to see *Groundhog Day* if you have not, it's a simple idea which raises lots of profound thoughts and questions. In the meantime – if you had to be trapped in the same day - which would you choose?

Who Won the Bronze?

Life isn't as tidy as we'd like it to be, I'm sure we all know that from our own experience. The movies, though, tidy it up for us. They have obvious villains and heroes and neat beginnings and conclusive endings (many of them anyway), but reality is different.

Much as I love *Chariots of Fire* – and I do really love it, it's been one of my favourite movies for years –- it doesn't tell the complete stories of Eric Liddell and Harold Abrahams, two British athletes at the 1924 Olympics. For one thing Eric Liddell knew months before he set foot on the ship to Paris that he wouldn't be running in the 100m because the heats were going to be held on a Sunday, and he refused to run on the Sabbath. In the movie he only discovers this as he is boarding the ship, and so wrestles with the issue whilst on the journey across the channel. In the film Abrahams mentions losing out in the 200m before he sets foot on the track to win the 100m final. In reality the 200m final was run *after* the 100m. It is to this day. But that would be an anti-climax. We want to see the film end with him and Liddell winning their races. And win they certainly did in dramatic, truly inspirational style.

Both Abrahams and Liddell had unusual running styles. Abrahams was coached by Sam Mussabini to run with his arms almost at right angles, and leaning forward. Liddell ran with his head back, as one recent BBC documentary put it, 'Looking to God.' When Ian Charleson trained to play the part of Eric Liddell in the movie he said the style reminded him of trust exercises he had done at drama school, and perhaps there was some essence of trust in Liddell's way of competing, honouring God with his running.

And so to real life and the 200 metres final in Paris, in 1924. Both Liddell and Abrahams lined up on the starting line, no blocks back then, just a trowel to dig a starting hole for your foot. They lined up with Charlie Paddock and Jackson Scholz, the two American runners who Abrahams had already beaten to win the 100m gold. As mentioned in the movie, in the 200m Abrahams was beaten 'out of sight'. He came last. So you've probably guessed it. Eric Liddell won the bronze medal, behind Scholz and Paddock. Though this is not referenced in the film.

The reason I mention it now is this. The stories of Liddell and Abrahams included coming last and third in the 200 metres final. Still incredible achievements. That was how their 1924 Olympic story ended. But it was not as tidy and complete and rousing as winning the gold medals in the 100m and 400m. So the film ended with those stories. Our day-to-day living is not like the movies, it does not have a nice, neat, tidy version of our lives, complete with rousing music just before the credits roll. We live with the realities of the highs and lows. You are probably great at something and rubbish at something else. If we ever write our autobiographies we may want to tidy the story and tell it a different way, but we don't need to. We are all a strange mixture of sludge and glory, mud and magnificence. The credits don't roll just as we make some fantastic achievement, instead we have to continue on, through the ordinary mire of the following day. The athletes we see competing so extraordinarily on our TV and computer screens have ordinary lives and troubles and families back home. They are real people, after all. You and I may never win a bronze medal, never mind the gold, but we don't need to cover it up or, as we might say now, airbrush the picture.

Sweeter than Space Dust

It was impossible to sit through Nigel Slater's *Life is Sweets* a while back and not be sugar-rushed back in time to those heady days of 1970s childhood confectionery. Black Jacks, Pineapple Cubes, Flying Saucers, Fruit Gums, American Hard Gums, Space Dust, Amazin Raisin and Aztec chocolate bars.

They all came rushing back, along with images of that village corner shop with row upon row of large sweetie jars, with their huge round lids, lids so big that adult hands were stretched to the limit as they swivelled them off. I used to catch the bus to school outside that sweet shop, and many Fruit Salads were bought there – well you could get four for a penny back then. (Aye, and you could get a three piece suit, a two course dinner and a packet of woodbines and still have change from thruppence.)

Last year, whilst on a bike ride on holiday, we came across an old-fashioned sweet shop where you could still buy chocolate cigarette sticks, complete with authentic-looking white rice paper wrapping. So we did. We bought some. I still have the empty pack, though the cigarettes are looooo-ng gone.

One of my strongest childhood sweet memories involves a Saturday morning, a Mars Bar and a copy of one of Richmal Crompton's *Just William* books. (From the library I think.) While my parents were still asleep I crept into the kitchen with the aforementioned Mars Bar -- a whole bar! -- and carefully cut it into small slices, with a fairly sharp knife, I think. (Mars Bars were tough in them days. They have since become softer I believe.) That done I returned to the haven of my bed, and carefully and deliberately chomped my way through the slivers of chocolate and toffee, whilst reading my book about the daring escapades of the first Will.I.Am and his mates. Who always seemed to end up in fist fights. Those stories seemed like a prototype for *Die Hard* sometimes. Bruce Willis in a ragged school cap and blazer, with a catapult and scuffed knees.

A couple of the writers of the Bible use sweet analogies. Guitar-playing King Dave, the mood-swing King who penned almost half of the rock songs in the book of Psalms, describes God's ways as being 'sweeter than honey' in Psalm 19. Ezra the priest does exactly the same in another of those songs – Psalm 119, verse 103. That particular track is an epic number, imagine *Bohemian Rhapsody* segued into *Stairway to Heaven* and that's about the size of it. And that's not including any guitar and drum solos. Both writers were saying that, as good and pleasing and satisfying as Pear Drops/Space Dust/Liquorice Allsorts/Black Jacks are, God's words of life satisfy your being on a whole other level. God's ways, they say, are even better than Heroes, Curly Wurlys, Bounties and Yorkies.

It's worth noting that honey itself was not always considered good. Proverbs chapter 25 verse 16 warns that 'too much honey will make you sick'. And later in the same chapter, in verse 25, we are told that 'it's not good to eat too much honey'. So it came with a health warning, you could say it was a 'guilty pleasure'. Not so the word of God, it's sweeter than honey (or Mars Bars) yet there are no calories in it.

So there you go, your sweet supply, that guilty pleasure, can be a useful reminder of the good things of God.

The Parable of the Blogger

Recently I have been doing various seminars and talks on the way folks in the Bible communicated. I am convinced that St Paul (the guy who sent those famous letters to the Corinthians, Ephesians, Galatians and Simpsons) would have loved the likes of Facebook and Twitter. He would have made very good use of this social networking malarkey to get the good news out to as many people as possible. He wouldn't have had to get on a boat, get shipwrecked and be bitten by a snake! All he needed was his tablet and Skype.

In his book *Whatever Happened to the Ark of the Covenant* Nick Page describes the way that the early Christians embraced the new technology of their day – namely Codices. Pieces of parchment chopped up and stitched together to effectively create the world's first paperbacks. Everyone else was still using scrolls to record their sacred writings, but not the Christians, they wanted something that was portable, easy to hide, and useful for jotting down copies of teaching, letters and parables.

Jesus loved stories. Tales of the unexpected, that were full of humour and twists and turns. He told many hugely entertaining and highly relevant parables. They were often his sermons. If he were around now I'm sure he would be telling other stories. Ones that are relevant to us now. Not so much the lost sheep -- but the lost pair of glasses. Not the poor widow and the unjust judge, but the homeless person and the corrupt politician.

Jesus once told the parable of the sower. Nowadays I am sure he would tell the parable of the blogger. The sower goes out and sows seeds all over the place, he's not really a great farmer, he just chucks the stuff everywhere, paths, rocks, soil, weeds. Jesus was describing his own approach – he had come to bring the good news to all sorts of unlikely people and places. So now I think he might talk about the blogger who takes the good news and hurls it across the internet, no idea where it might land and where it might bear some fruit. The good stuff goes out like the farmer's seeds. And though many discard it and some trample on it, while others overlook it, in some places it strikes a chord and finds a home and develops into new life.

I spoke about this recently in a church service, and afterwards I chatted with a young guy who told me he had used a pool table as a parable about the way Jesus worked. There are probably all kinds of everyday kind of things that would make useful parables. Maybe you can think of a few new retellings yourself. Worth chewing on...

Like a Magic Eye Picture

Our daughter is just getting into those magic eye pictures, or stereograms. This requires sitting oddly close to the page of a book or, in her case a computer screen, until you go cross-eyed and then suddenly you see something you've never spotted before hidden in the picture. The image takes on whole new dimensions. Objects appear to float off the page and the thing comes to life, no longer merely a flat picture. Don't worry if you’ve tried this and can't see them – it can give you a headache or just drive you plain mad, especially when others are enthusiastically telling you how easy it is to fathom them.

I think the faith is a bit like that. You can debate it, reason it, chew on it, but ultimately something else, something extra, has to happen – I would call it the work of God's spirit – when suddenly you see what you could not see before. Other things come into focus. The picture comes alive, and you are never the same again. Jesus called these other things 'the secrets of the kingdom' and he wrapped them up in parables. These were like his own magic eye pictures, and he left them for us to contemplate and absorb – three-dimensional stories full of wisdom and hope and life. They are there for us to keep chewing on, but unlike magic eye pictures, they don’t simply just come alive once. They are full of layers, and year on year we may revisit them and discover hidden depths whenever we take the time.

But, whatever you do, don't stretch the analogy too far, don’t take your ability to fathom magic eye pictures as any indication of your depth of faith. Whether or not you can make any sense of stereograms isn't an indicator of your state as a proper Christian!!! It's just a useful parable...

Coming From the Wrong Place

I have been continually frustrated by my lack of ability to put a comedy place name in my Facebook profile. I would love to record that I live in Neverland, or Middle Earth or Narnia or Discworld but they are just not allowed. I wanted to put somewhere creative and comical but Facebook would not play ball. So I felt somewhat vindicated when I heard this item on the news. Folks who live in a place in Ireland called Effin are not allowed to put in their real actual place of dwelling because Facebook is too strict!! Presumably second-guessing that this is a shortened form of a rather rude word.

Jesus may have sympathised with the folks from Effin. After all, people made gags about his hometown, Nazareth, the place of no-hopers. It was seen as a bit of a backwater, and when a guy called Nathanael bumped into Jesus one day he made a telling comment, 'Can anything good come from Nazareth?' Well, he was to spend the next three years finding out.

Jesus's ancestry goes back to a little place that is now famous because of festive carols and Cliff Richard, but at the time Bethlehem was not up to much really. Hardly the Big Apple of the Bible. Incidentally, a friend told me some time ago that Bethlehem means 'house of bread' – which kind of means that Jesus, who called himself 'the bread of life', was born in a bakery! I like that. And people say the Bible has no humour in it.

Jesus should have been born in Jerusalem of course. Not only the home of the temple, but the city of God. That surely would have looked much better in his Facescroll profile. Because it was the home of the temple everyone believed that God lived there, deep inside the holy building. However, Jesus spent more time in other places. In the downtowns and backwaters, away from the action and the lights. When he was growing up and working with his dad, he may well have spent time in Sephoris. A city of celebrity and culture, the place had been sacked by the Romans and needed a lot of rebuilding. Well, Jesus could have chosen Sephoris for his ministry, it was a boom town of culture and trade, not too far from Nazareth. He may well have done a lot of work there over the years. But once he changed career from carpenter to rabbi he didn't pay any visits.

When Jesus did take the time to visit Jerusalem, he often caused controversy. The temple there was full of gates, and at each gate more people were excluded. At the first gate the gentiles (non-Jews) had to stop, at the next gate the women had to stop, at the next gate the men, then the priests, until, at the final gate, only the High Priest for that year could go through and get into what was called The Holy of Holies. This was the place to meet with God. And each year only one man was allowed to go inside and do this. Jesus changed all that, he pinched the gate analogy for himself and basically said, 'I am the gate and now anyone can go through. No one has to stop. The invitation is open to all.' (See John chapter 10 verse 9.) Jesus brought a whole new system, one of invitation, rather than exclusion, very different to the temple. This was a brand new way of meeting with God, and one that was on offer to all. Anyone could now go through the gate and meet the Creator.

No Hollywood Endings

I was chatting with a mate last night about the film *500 Days of Summer*, and the way the movie does not turn out to have a romantically happy ending (sorry to spoil it there for you). It started me thinking about the way Jesus's blockbuster stories often don't end with a smile and a Disney song by Tim Rice and Elton John.

Jesus tells lots of stories, and they would have made good films, but his parables don't often end well... in fact, just when you think a happy ending is on the way – bam! It all turns dark.

There's a rich man who has been blessed by God and been given a bumper crop. At first he won't share his money and simply invests in bigger storage buildings, but then he rethinks and shares it with the neighbourhood... or does he? Nope. He dies suddenly and tragically, surrounded by newly-constructed barns. Presumably no one came to his funeral (Luke 12). Then there are the greedy tenants who take over a farm and refuse to give it up. The owner sends messengers to try and get them to see sense but they refuse. So finally the owner sends his own son and the tenants realise their folly and things turn out fine and dandy... or do they? Nope. They cruelly murder the son, rub their hands with glee and then promptly get slaughtered by the owner's hitmen. Presumably no one came to their funerals either (Luke 20).

Then there is the wedding crasher who sneaks into the marriage feast thrown by a king for his son. Having refused to come when the invitations were sent out he decides to go on his own terms, without a proper wedding outfit, sneaks over the back fence and clambers his way in through a window. The groom sees him, applauds his change of mind, gives him a shirt and tie and hands him a glass of the finest red. Or does he? Nope. He is grabbed by a couple of heavies and thrown enthusiastically into outer darkness where he sobs uncontrollably and grinds his teeth forever. Sob sob, grind grind (Matthew 22).

And as if that isn't enough, there is carnage in the middle of this parable too. When all those invited refuse to come (some of them killing the messengers when a simple 'No thanks' would have probably done the job) they are then slaughtered by the king's men, who also burn their cities to a crisp. In the film *Dogville* there is a scene reminiscent of this. Grace visits a village and is abused and rejected there. So her father shows up and takes his violent revenge. Interestingly, Grace wants to forgive but her gangster daddy has other plans.

And then there's the servant who is forgiven a massive, whopping great debt, but can't forgive others and so gets thrown into prison and the whole sorry tale ends with a torture scene (Matthew 18).

Hmm. Not sure the Disney bosses will go for any of this. It's certainly a lot more Tarantino than *Toy Story*.

Even the world famous, ever popular, runaway boy adventure – The Prodigal Son – doesn't end with a nod and a wink and a knees-up-Mother-Brown. Instead, just when it's all looking rosy, there's a lengthy scene involving a slanging match with the older brother who storms off, slamming the door on his way out. Roll the Credits.

My friend was telling me that the reason *500 Days of Summer* ends like it does, is that it's part of a new breed of romantic comedies which, instead of just being pure escapism where the guy and the girl get each other, deal with something closer to reality. *500 Days* even goes as far as to show you what the guy would love to happen, but then contrasts it with what really happens. Not unlike our lives.

And that's where Jesus's adventures come in. They are by no means tales of escapism, though they do feature humour, action, violence, suspense and the unexpected. These are tales which reflect reality. Take for example one of my favourites, the drama about the credit-crunch stricken widow, and the filthy rich celebrity, oh sorry, I mean the filthy rich judge. The woman is desperately poor and needs justice, she begs and begs for help but the judge couldn't care less. Ever feel like that? Overlooked? Locked out in the cold? Ever scared that you'll be lost with nothing? Ever have money worries? This is a tale for our time – it taps into all those feelings and situations. The big picture in this story is one of encouragement to persevere and pray and not lose heart, to keep on being hopeful and faithful. But the power of the story for me is in the detail. The difficulties of the woman.

I think Jesus understands that most of us have days when we feel that life or God are unjust; and days when we fear, having blown it yet again, that God will judge us harshly. Maybe even punish us in some way. So we find the figure of God in this story is represented, or perhaps misrepresented, by a harsh, uncaring judge. Jesus seems to be saying, 'Even though your picture of God can get skewed, keep going. Don't give up.'

This is powerful, honest stuff. The story is not just an unsympathetic command to keep praying and believing, we all struggle with that, it's an insight into why we may struggle to do that, struggle to believe, struggle to keep hoping. Jesus has the insight to see all of this.

These stories may be dark but they also give us room to manoeuvre, they don't demand an impossible kind of lifestyle, or an escapist faith, instead they tap into reality and help us to earth who we are as we wrestle with what we believe.

I'm as Intimate as a Concrete Block

A couple of things have set me thinking about the whole issue of intimacy. It's still very popular in some church circles to talk about intimacy with God, but I have a sackful of questions about that whole thing.

Firstly, my main reference for intimacy has to be my relationship with my wife (feel free to substitute cuddly toy/boyfriend/girlfriend/husband/chocolate/gnome/ dog/cat/cushion/hot-buttered toast/stick insect for that – all comers are welcome here). Intimacy with my wife involves the five senses -- taste, touch, smell, sight and sound (in case you have a few others) – and none of these really plays much part in my relationship with God. I may admittedly hear and see signs of God and his ways in the world around, but I wouldn't think of that as being intimacy.

Secondly, men are pretty rubbish at intimacy. Don't believe me? Well, it's hardly proof but I'm currently reading an entertaining, insightful and very well observed book called *Watching the English* by Kate Fox (she spent a long time deliberately queue jumping, bumping into other people and watching guys in pubs for research). It's all about the unspoken laws of operation of those on this small island. When discussing men and their pub talk, Kate Fox makes a throwaway comment where she says – 'Men are terrified of intimacy' – which is why they use insults, banter and arguments to communicate. I think there's a huge amount of truth in this, we men struggle with the rawness of reality, don't we? We seem to manage brief flashes of it, when we are particularly vulnerable, or after a few beers, or perhaps if someone else starts the ball rolling... but I think she has a point. I know it when I consider my own shortcomings here.

And this leads to my third point. Are we substituting this idea of 'intimacy with God' for intimacy with others. Bearing in mind how much easier it is to bear my soul with an invisible Creator, someone who won't hold out on me, or dismiss me, or ignore me or misunderstand me. It may be that we long to be more open with others but it's too risky, too costly, been too damaging in the past, or like me, you just seem to not have that gene. One of my frustrations with some Christian meetings is that I wish they were places of more reality, and yet I don't even know where to begin with that...

I'm not really saying that this idea of intimacy with God is right or wrong, just that I'm not sure what we can really expect and what people really mean when they talk of this. God is 'other', he is not like us, he invites us to follow Jesus and live differently. Plus, the danger here is that we may sometimes imagine that others have a depth of intimacy with God that is in reality beyond our reach. And that may therefore leave us feeling inadequate and second best, because we don't seem able to achieve it.

I'll leave the last thought on this subject to the prophet Jeremiah, who wrote something like this: 'If there is anything to talk of, anything to boast about, let it be this – that we know the living God, and understand that he is righteous, just and loving' (Jeremiah chapter 9 verse 24).

Ordinary

I try and blog something hugely profound a few times a week, something that will shake Christendom to its core. But this morning I'm stuck. Reminds me of the opening to Adrian Plass's legendary *Sacred Diary* which begins with the immortal lines: 'Felt led to keep a diary. A sort of spiritual log for the benefit of others... each new divine insight will shine like a beacon in the darkness. Can't think of anything to put in today.'

I re-read it recently and it still makes me laugh out loud.

So, with that in mind I've jumped to a few thoughts that have been rattling around like stray marbles in the tobacco tin of my brain for a while. I was thinking about how we know so little of the 30 years when Jesus was growing up. We know about the remarkable circumstances surrounding his birth, and then we jump 12 years to a quick visit to the temple, then we jump another 18 and find ourselves at the start of the big adventure, the three action-jammed years of Jesus's life that resemble a sort of biblical version of *The Bourne Ultimatum*, with a lot more jokes thrown in.

But what about the years in between? What were his first words as a child – mummy, daddy, or blessed are the meek? What about the toddler tantrums and the birthdays and the gum-chewing teenage mood swings and the learning to chisel and the hitting-the-thumb-with-a-hammer moments. The years of boom and bust and credit crunch and high Roman taxation, the long days working in nearby boom town Sephoris. Where are the details and why are they missing?

I have often joked that there's very little because Mary and Joseph grounded Jesus after the temple incident in Jerusalem. That time when they started the long journey home to Nazareth while Jesus had snuck back to banter with the bigwigs. When his mum and dad found out he was missing, they ran back, cuffed his ear and said, 'You're not going out again for the next 18 years!'

But the truth is probably, thankfully, less profound. No one recorded those years because they were most likely unremarkable. Extremely ordinary. Like our lives. Jesus grew up and did the kind of things that every normal person does. He certainly had humble beginnings because his parents were not affluent. If there was anything remarkable about his early life it was the fact that he grew up in an oppressed country. Like Burma or North Korea. He had to cope with the stress of living in a country occupied by the brutal Romans.

One of the things we often find hardest to settle in our heads is the ordinariness of the son of God. It's the reason so many pictures of Jesus show him wearing a halo. We want a shiny powerful *X Factor* Jesus, solving the world's snags with an X Box full of quick-fix miracles. An iPod messiah. The true miracle of the son of God is that he understands what our lives are like because he has dared to live as a human himself.

I like this bit in Paul's email to the Philippians, chapter 2 verses 5 to 7:
'Your attitude should be the same that Jesus had. Though he was God, he did not demand and cling to his rights as God. He made himself nothing; he took the humble position of a slave and appeared in human form.'

That's something – the God who disguises himself as a slave. Not a Superman God but a servant king. And having lived 30 normal years in a quiet, poor family, he was then well prepared to relate to those he met who were crushed, disappointed, lost and searching. As well as those living normal, ordinary lives. Like you and me.

'This High Priest of ours understands our weaknesses, for he faced all of the same temptations we do, yet he did not sin. So let us come boldly to the throne of our gracious God. There we will receive his mercy, and we will find grace to help us when we need it.' So says the writer of the email to the Hebrews in chapter 4 verses 15 and 16.

Stuck in the Middle

Do you ever feel as if you are caught between two worlds? I'll try and explain why I ask that. I sometimes come across material and messages from Christians who are desperate to prove the faith with stories and dogmatic statements of theology... and I'm sad that we feel we have to fight our corner like this.

And then I watch TV and I hear Stephen Fry say on *QI* that the story of Mary and Joseph going to Bethlehem at Christmas is 'Poppycock' – because there never was a census. And I'm annoyed and frustrated that those outside the faith seem so keen and happy when they can declare their proof that Christianity is not real in some way. When will we ever learn that faith is not about proof, has nothing to do with proof, and our arguments about this are futile. Faith has much more to do with relationship and trust.

I'm sad that some Christians feel the need to prove that they are right, waving the faith around like a dangerous weapon, and understandably some non-Christians take every chance to shoot back. Both sides then appearing to be desperate to prove they are right.

I like what Don Miller says in his book *Blue Like Jazz*:
'Sooner or later you just figure out that there are some folks who don't believe in God and they can prove that he doesn't exist, and some guys who do believe in God and they can prove he does exist, and the argument stopped being about God a long time ago and now it's about who is smarter, and honestly I don't care. I don't believe I will ever walk away for intellectual reasons. Who knows anything anyway? If I walk away from him, and please pray that I never do, it will be for

social reasons, identity reasons, deep emotional reasons, the same reasons any of us do anything.'

I like this. I really like it. I think this is wise stuff. So often I try and argue for the faith on an intellectual level, forgetting that most of the time we react to things because of our personalities and experience and troubles. I was chatting recently to a young Christian (wow! – that makes me sound old!) and he said that most people are not walking round wondering about God and his place in their life. So I asked him what our job was as Christians. He said, 'To be a caring community.'

Bang! Suddenly we're back with Jesus and his heartfelt prayer for us, 'This is how people will know it's real – if they care for each other.'
A couple of years ago I read an interview with Ben Elton (in *Third Way* magazine) in which the interviewer asked, 'What are you trying to make people think with your writing?' to which Ben Elton replied, 'I'm not trying to make them think anything, I'm trying to make myself think.'

It struck me then that so much of my 'christian' communication is made up of carefully constructed words designed to change other people. Even when I pray out loud in public meetings my prayers are mini-sermons attempting to alter other peoples' thinking, when I should be speaking to myself, I'm the one with so much that needs changing. Why is it so easy to see the minor faults in others and miss the gaping wounds in myself?

How can I be different? How can I react differently? How can I be an answer to Jesus's prayer when most of the time I'm really just an introspective, injured coward? Hmm.

Everyone's Unbalanced

We're all unbalanced. And quite right too. I lean towards the earthy side of life, often saying things that are perhaps inappropriate, but helpful because other people are sometimes thinking those things but would not say them. I am also on the side of the God who is approachable, connected with earthy reality. The God who made himself accessible and small. I need folks who will remind me of the awesome nature of God, the holiness of God. Recently my dad said to me, 'God is bigger and smaller than we expect.' I like that.

It is sometimes tempting to believe we should all be a lot more balanced, a lot more like one another. But I don't think so. We are all uniquely made, with our own stories, our own personalities, our own strengths and weaknesses. And that makes us biased. Which is why we need one another. That's why we're in this thing together. To share strengths and weaknesses and to bring balance. Together, a group of unbalanced people, we bring the balance required. That's what a community is about. We bring balance by being more ourselves and getting together with others who are different. We don't need to be like-minded, we just need to be in agreement. And there's a difference.

Imagine two athletes, a weightlifter and a cyclist. Both throw themselves into the sport they love, they may well also draw on other disciplines to help them train, but no one expects the cyclist to try and be a brilliant weightlifter and vice versa. They are supposed to work on their individual gifts, to develop different skills and express them. Not become more balanced by doing lots of sports. They are supposed to go as far as they can with their own calling. That's how it works. So it is with us as people. The danger of trying to be balanced is that we end up being mediocre. And at times that is how I feel. When I am more concerned about what others might think of me, rather than what God desires. I side towards mediocrity, toning down the gifts I have, reigning in the personality God has given me. I'm not saying we should all be belligerent and uncaring towards others, just steamrollering on and being insensitive towards those who are different. But neither should we all pretend we are the same, and hide ourselves away for the sake of being nice.

When three men were given talents in a story Jesus told, the two who really went for it, and spent themselves in order to make something, were highly commended. The one who buried his gifts and played it safe got his knuckles rapped.

We may rattle cages, and rock boats by being ourselves, we're bound to, and things may seem a lot more pleasant when we all try and be the same, and nod nicely. But we must not be afraid of who we are. If I am unbalanced in one direction, and you are unbalanced in the opposite way, then in coming together we create a whole. Surely we attain balance not by all being the same, but by coming together with other unbalanced people. We need each other for that very reason. I am fearfully and wonderfully made, and so are you. But God used different patterns when he wired us up.

Sunday Blues

I still find church services really difficult. I have always found them so, ever since I was a wee lad. There was a period in the 1980s, when I was moving in charismatic circles, when I enjoyed the extensive worship singing. But that's quite a while ago now, and there has been much water under the ecclesiastical bridge.

A few years ago I read that some men find going to church a bit like going to school, which is why they find it difficult. I didn't particularly enjoy school, so that may explain my discomfort somewhat. I'm afraid I just find myself getting bored, distracted and frustrated as the time goes on. And I also feel oddly isolated. I'm just not good at being sociable.

I banged on about this problem in some detail a few years ago when I wrote the book *The Bloke's Bible*, but some of the fevers and struggles of that period have now passed. However, the mistake I continue to make is that I expect church to be easier now. It isn't. A while ago a friend and I attended a carol service where we were due to perform some drama. I noticed that the youngster in the pew in front of us was painstakingly ticking off each carol as we sang it. That's me. That's what I'm like, not so much in carol services (I actually do enjoy carols) but in church in general, I am mentally ticking off each item as it moves me towards the end of things. (Not the end of everything, although that too moves closer with every passing service, just the end of that particular church experience.)

These days I am often speaking or leading church services and that does make it easier. Probably because I have some control. Plus having input makes me both more nervous and more engaged. And I do tend to find that helps. This all sounds terribly judgmental, and I am aware that so many folks get a huge amount out of church services. So I recognise this is my issue. There was a time when I would have blamed church per se, and whilst I do think that many services would benefit from a more diverse creative approach, and the language could be much more down to earth, with less christianese, I realise it's really my problem.

It doesn't matter whether the church services are lively or not, in fact I tend to enjoy short, quieter services these days. Half an hour with a couple of hymns, a contemporary sermon, and some liturgy would do me fine really. (Don't demand much, do I??) There was a time when I loved the 'modern choruses', but now they tend to annoy me because they bang on about me and God, what I'm going to do for him, and how I feel about him. The biblical picture is much more about the nature of God, and the collective people of God (to quote *High School Musical* 'We're all in this together!'). We often forget that many of the you's in the Bible are plural.

Plus of course biblical worship is about a way of life, loving God with all our minds, wills, souls, strength and hearts. Not just a collection of songs with good tunes. When Micah was quizzed about the best things people can offer to God, he swept aside the traditional expectations of the best quality sacrifices in organised corporate worship, and instead opted for lives that were seeking to live with the strands of justice, mercy and humility woven through them. Jeremiah told the people that God wanted them to know this, 'I don't want your burnt offerings – eat 'em yourself!' (Jeremiah chapter 7 verse 21). Isaiah went further and told the people that true worship is caring for those in society who are marginalised, poor, overlooked (Isaiah chapter 58). It seems that the people had become confused, they were putting a lot of effort into sacrificing animals and staging elaborate worship events, but their lives did not reflect their vocal dedication to God.

Add to this mix verse one from the email to the Romans, in chapter 12, which invites us to bring our lives as a living sacrifice, and you get the picture. For the Romans who read the email this was shocking stuff, they'd only ever seen dead sacrifices, dripping with blood and bodily fluids and placed on an altar for burning. This was a new era, an era we still live in now, an era where sacrifice wasn't about doing violence to other creatures, but about bringing our cluttered, clumsy living to God for him to make something useful out of the chaos.

I came up with my own description of worship and it's this:
Worship is warming God's heart.
I wonder what you do that warms God's heart?

It seems to me that Sunday church should be a time that inspires, equips and informs us about how to worship God for the rest of our week in our living, labouring, laughing and loving. (And in our alliteration of course.)

All of this complaining puts me in the frame as little more than a religious Victor Meldrew, and I’d put my hand up to that, but maybe there is some truth in my griping. Whinge over. For now.

It’ll no doubt resurface next Sunday. ☺

Dark Dinosaurs

A few years back I went to see a film called *Tyrannosaur* with a friend, and let me tell you, a romantic comedy it was not. Neither does it have anything to do with *Jurassic World*. It's written and directed by a guy called Paddy Considine (on TV he played Mr Whicher in *The Suspicions of Mr Whicher*) and it's what you might call a brutal British drama. It tells the story of Joseph, a lonely, ravaged man, plagued by violence and his past. One day, while attempting to flee from his own rage he runs and hides in a charity shop, and there he meets Hannah (played by Olivia Colman). Hannah believes in God and this quickly becomes apparent when she tries to help him and prays one of the most genuine and 'real' prayers I've seen on the big screen. It's very hard to portray good people on the silver screen without it turning into solid cinematic syrup, but this is something Olivia Colman does incredibly well indeed. She also happens to play Tom Hollander's wife in the TV series *Rev*.

Tyrannosaur is not a happy film, and be warned – the language is stronger than a slab of Wensleydale left in the sun for three weeks – let's just say the swearing is occasionally peppered with ordinary words. Many of the characters are caught up in aggressive, difficult lifestyles, including the middle-class Hannah. This is brutal 18-rated soap opera stuff, and I came out reeling from some of the scenes and disturbed by the sad reality of these peoples' lives.

Hannah's life at first appears to be happy and privileged. But as the film unfolds we discover other things. And this may disturb us – if you're like me you want stories where the

Christians are sorted, positive people who spend all day making a difference in the world.

The gap between what we would like life and Christians to be, and the reality of what life and Christians are like, can unsettle us. And hey – we are probably most aware of this gap in our own lives. We want to live out shiny, all-our-prayers-answered, happy-ever-afters, we want to be people who get converted and live the rest of our lives as uber-saints. People can look at Christians and somehow expect them to be perfect and successful – there's an awful lot of pressure to be St Paul in jeans. Even though St Paul was far from perfect and admitted it. With or without his jeans. (Check out his biblical email to the Romans, chapter 7.)

However, trouble is a shared language –- we can all speak it, Christian or not – and what we discover in this movie is that in spite of her problems and struggles Hannah is still able to help Joseph. The writers of the Bible sometimes describe people as being sons and daughters of dust. That's how we are described in Psalm 103 verse 14. In other words, God knows he's dealing with the wreckage of our lives when he takes us on. We may disappoint ourselves and others with our high expectations, but we cannot disappoint him. Jesus calls us to follow and he knows the kind of baggage we may bring along for the ride. He's seen it all.

Why is Christianity a Bit Like Bat Out of Hell?

Back in the dark days of 1975 two guys met in a room and began to bash out some tunes. They spent ages crafting each song very carefully indeed. The two guys were Meat Loaf and his mate Jim Steinman and the result was an album of seven tracks entitled *Bat Out of Hell.*

They spent two years trying to get a recording contract. No one was very interested. Apart from an engineer called Todd Rundgren. He believed in the project and mixed and recorded the album for them and then started looking for a record label. They tried 30. Yes, 30 record labels.

Nothing. Zilch. Zero.
No one wanted to know.
It was dead in the water. The bat might as well just sneak back into hell. It had no future.

Enter a small record label called Cleveland records. They signed the album having only heard the first minute of one track. They released a single off their new album. Nothing happened. Still no one was interested. Tumbleweed drifted past. They released a second single. More tumbleweed. They released a third. More tumbleweed. More people not interested. No one could give a bat's ass. Then MTV came along, and fortunately Todd Rundgren made a video of Mr Loaf, or Meat as his friends might call him. MTV needed videos and they played it.

It's nearly 40 years later and *Bat Out of Hell* is the fifth most successful album of all time. It stayed on the U.K. chart for 474 weeks. It has sold 43 million copies the world over. It still sells approximately 200,000 copies each year.

An album no one wanted to record and no one wanted to sell. What does this have to do with Christianity?
Well, it's not an unusual story, Van Gogh didn't sell a painting while he was alive, though he once swapped one for a pint of beer. JK Rowling couldn't find a publisher. Sometimes you just cannot tell what will grow and what will not.

When Jesus slipped off this mortal coil and melted back into the kingdom of heaven he left behind a handful of followers in a struggling country. Having once fed thousands of people he ended up with a fraction of that number and most of them were scared stupid. He had established no training programme, no school of divinity, he left no Alpha Course and no Purpose Driven Book.

Yet today there are approximately 2 billion followers of Jesus in the world.
2 billion. Can you picture that? I can't.
Every day thousands of people hear the call of Jesus and start to follow him. What began as a tiny Jewish sect in a beleaguered country has defied all the odds and all the logic and grown to be the biggest religion in the world. In spite of the fact that the founder warned his followers that the future would be tough for them and he himself was murdered as a criminal.

I was recently chatting to a guy and I asked him why he had become a Christian, what had pushed him over the edge? He told me that he had been so impressed with those first followers, in particular those first eleven disciples who had been willing to die for their faith. None had given up. Today you and I can trace our spiritual ancestry to those eleven.

You just cannot tell what will die and what will flourish.

Imagine That?

Who would have thought that? One of John Lennon's teeth selling for ten thousand pounds. Amazing!
Of course it's nothing new – bits of the great and the good being highly valued. Elvis Presley's nasal douche (!) was part of an auction summer sale in 2009. Seems we all want a bit of celebrity shrapnel. Even stuff from their medicine cabinet...

In the early days people wanted bits of Jesus and his mates. Pieces of bone and bits of cloth and other artefacts did the rounds and ended up in churches all over the place. Not sure if anyone ever claimed to have Thomas's wisdom tooth, but you never know. I heard recently that one possible idea for Spielberg's next Indiana Jones movie is the hunt for the cross of Jesus. In reality of course the Romans would have most likely re-used it, these things were just every day tools for Caesar's slaughter squads.

I do like the artefact moment in *Indiana Jones and the Last Crusade* though, the moment where they think they've discovered the cup Jesus used at the last supper. When offered a selection of possible cups the bad guys immediately reach for the most impressive, jewel studded cup. And pay the price. By contrast Dr Jones goes for a battered old cup – 'the cup of a carpenter' – not an expensive diamond encrusted thing. I like that because it points us back to the normality and poverty of Jesus's life. He came from a simple background, his parents were certainly not well off. When they dedicated him in the temple they brought the cheapest offering, two young pigeons. It's also worth noting that when Mary made up her song to celebrate being pregnant she pointed out that God had lifted up the poor and brought down the rich. That's a bit of a clue to her own status really.

But back to that artefact, finding Jesus in a battered old cup reminds me that he is found in the ordinary places. Big old cathedrals are all right but you can just as easily bump into him in a communal loo in the slums of Nairobi. Or in the chores and the normality of Monday to Friday. Jesus stepped into real life. And spent much of his time amongst the everyday.

I've always been a bit of a fan of the Turin Shroud, the possible burial cloth of Jesus. I just find the whole thing fascinating, especially as no one is really sure how the image got onto the cloth. One theory claims that it could have been a sudden huge burst of energy, not unlike the first big bang. If that's true then the resurrection is, as Tom Wright might say, the new Genesis. The new beginning of the world.

Ultimately you could say that people are the real artefacts of God. Jesus left us no selfies, except the ragtag bunch of followers we see around today. We're God's selfies. God's artefacts. Living, breathing, sweating, fretting saints. More valuable than a diamond encrusted cup, or a piece of cloth or an ancient splinter.

Let's Talk About Text

Just enjoying Nick Page's book, *God's Dangerous Book*, all about the way the Bible came into being. There's a great little strapline on the back which sums it up – 'The Bible was not delivered whole, shrink-wrapped and Jiffy-bagged onto the desk of St Paul by some heavenly FedEx courier.'

In 2011 we celebrated 400 years of the King James Bible, but that version came to us via various other translations. It wasn't as if old King J himself sat down one day, a little bit bored whilst waiting for *Countdown* to come on, and decided to turn all the Hebrew and Greek into English in one afternoon. Loads of people were working hard from a variety of motivations to bring the Bible to the average man in the field.

On his website (nickpage.co.uk/front-page-books/gods-dangerous-book) Nick quotes Gandhi, who read the Bible and said this:
"You Christians look after a document containing enough dynamite to blow all civilisation to pieces, turn the world upside down and bring peace to a battle-torn planet. But you treat it as though it is nothing more than a piece of literature."

A few years ago people kept telling me I would enjoy *Velvet Elvis* by Rob Bell. Me being me, I put off reading it because everybody else was talking about it. When I did finally humble myself and listen to the advice it began to radically change the way I read the Bible. Rob's writing put me onto Tom Wright (ex-Bishop of Durham and author of the *...For Everyone* series).

Reading these writers taught me a lot of things, but a few thoughts stand out.

First, understanding the context and the culture of the time changes our depth of understanding, and our vision of God, but often we need help from those who have done the research, like Nick, Tom and Rob. Just reading the Bible on our own will not always enable us to get it all. Secondly different bits of the Bible are related to other bits, e.g. the prodigal son parable and the tale of Jacob and Esau in Genesis chapter 27; the rich fool parable and Nabal and Abigail in 1 Samuel chapter 25; the great banquet and the character of Wisdom in the book of Proverbs chapter 9. And thirdly, the Bible contains a lot more humour and shocking material than you might think. The jokes of course are all cultural and of their time, but there are plenty in there.

In the beginning the Bible was a collection of stories told orally, with storytellers passing on the sacred text – and it seems to me that we live in an age where that kind of Bible-telling is once again highly relevant. Hearing the Bible and seeing it re-enacted on stage or film are vital in an age where so many people receive their information in a visual format.

What was once a heavy leather-backed book is now in digital format on my phone, tablet and desk top computer. It's in paperback form on my bookshelves, but I rarely open those. Nowadays a couple of clicks on my Bible and I'm reading the relevant bits. I can also Google any version of the Bible and be reading it in seconds. If I go to Blueletterbible.org I can read any word or sentence in the English and/or the Hebrew and the Greek, with extra explanation as to its meaning. Abraham and Paul would be amazed. Abraham went into the unknown with no sacred text, just a voice in the night.

In just a few short years since the invention of the World Wide Web, the internet has made every version of the Bible available to anyone with access to Wi-Fi.

The Bible always was the living, active word of God. More than ever now it is out there in the ether, waiting to be discovered afresh.

Keep Calm and Get Uptight

Okay, I'm a little confused. But firstly I'm amazed. I'm amazed at how quickly this wartime epitaph has spread like... well... one of those viral videos about a little boy and his bitten finger. I guess the times are hard, no doubt about that, so it's fitting really. It's very tempting to worry about tomorrow right now. We're all bombarded with news, news, news. The news itself thinks it's so important. You must watch it, you must hear about the bad things, again and again and again. You must, you must, you must! You'll be so miserable if you don't hear about all the terrible things going on in the world. So, when something like *Keep Calm...* comes along, that's a pretty good thing. A sort of latter day 'Do not worry about tomorrow...' So I can't complain.

However.

We spent a week making cappuccinos at New Wine a few summers ago, and a very good time it was too. But I just can't help myself. You see, the place was awash with a couple of things. Firstly – great people. Fantastic people. The best. So that was excellent. But it was also awash with christian stuff. If there is such a thing. Hang on, I'll just check Genesis.

'And on the ninth day, fresh from his day off, God made christian stuff...' No I don't think it's in the good book, but I'll move hastily on. (Especially as I write books to be sold as part of the christian stuff...)

The thing that got up my nose and down my goat was the following t-shirt slogan. Apologies if you possess one, it's really nothing personal. I hope it fits and keeps you warm

and does all the right things in all the right places. It's just... well... this: WHAT ON EARTH DOES IT MEAN?
***Keep PSALM and Carry On*?**
Er... how... what... where's the grammar? Where's the logic? Where's the door, I'll get my coat...

I don't mind us tapping into relevant culture and all that, of course not. It's a great idea. Jesus did it. Paul did it. The prophets did it. But if we're going to do it, can we please make it mean something. There could of course be a grammatical error, an epitaphical typo and an 'a' could be missing, i.e. Keep **a** psalm and carry on. But even cutting the t-shirts that kind of slack – which psalm should I keep? And where should I keep it? Under the bed? In my shoe? Behind my ear? All suggestions will be gratefully received, as long as they make sense and are not on your t-shirt.

Calm is an adjective. As far as I am aware, psalm is not. It's a noun.

So I'll get down off my pedantic, self-righteous, high horse now, and say have a good day and er... keep calm/psalm/lip-balm/Emmerdale-farm/uncle-Tom and carry/Barry/marry/tarry/doolally on. (Delete as the mood takes you.)

P.S. Since writing this rant I have come across another take on the *Keep Calm* slogan, relating to Psalm 37 verse 7:
Keep Calm... and Know That I Am God.

Now that makes sense.

Pregnant Prophets

I am fascinated by the pregnant prophets. Men and women in the Bible who carried their messages in their bodies and let it shape their living. Ezekiel, Hosea, Esther, Isaiah, Micah, Noah, Jeremiah, Ruth, John the Baptist. All of these shaped their lives around the message they carried inside them, implanted there by the God they loved and worshipped. Ezekiel locked himself in his house then dug his way out through the wall, Hosea knowingly married a promiscuous woman, Esther joined a harem, Isaiah and Micah went round naked, Noah built a boat in the middle of nowhere, Jeremiah bought pottery and smashed it up, Ruth left everything that was familiar to her, John lived in a wilderness. When a woman is pregnant it shapes her diet, her activities, her way of life, her decision making. She is very aware of the precious life she carries inside. So with these prophets.

In recent years we've seen folks like Dave Gorman and Danny Wallace come along, comedians who have lived strange lives for a while and then made shows and written books about them. Dave Gorman travelled far and wide to find another 52 people called Dave Gorman. Danny Wallace decided to say 'Yes' to everything for a year. He then started a cult by posting an advert in a national newspaper which invited people to 'Join me' just to see what would happen. Thousands responded and this became his cult of *Random Acts of Kindness* with a huge band of followers dedicated to making the world a nicer place.

Author A J Jacobs went more biblical – trying to follow all the rules of the Bible for a year. This included trying to stone people occasionally (only with tiny pebbles, they barely noticed), checking all his clothes for those dreaded mixed fibres, and not going near his wife or anything she had touched when she was having her period. (You can imagine how well that went down! His wife insisted on touching everything in the house so in the end he had to carry his own seat round with him.) But he also learnt some interesting stuff about praying and giving away. He then went on to write *The Year of Living Biblically.*

I guess all the writers of the Bible did this kind of thing. Lived unusual lives for a while and recorded what happened. Then like Danny Wallace, they effectively said, 'Join me' to see how many others would follow their way.

Ultimately Jesus carried his calling inside of him for 30 years, waiting for the right moment to start living it out. And three years after that his life produced the ultimate new birth, when in dying and resurrecting, his life multiplied and touched billions of followers all over the globe.

It's costly though. These pregnant prophets often paid a price for their counter cultural lifestyles. Jesus himself said that it was in dying that a seed produced a harvest of new life. And some of them gave everything in order to leave their legacy.

We still see them today, these pregnant prophets. Women and men who are willing to live differently as they carry within them the grace and good news of God, taking it to those who need it.

Exclusive!
New Beatitude Discovered after 2000 Years!!

Actually I've found four. Amazing! You wait for a new one for 2000 years and then four come along all at once! If you have a look at Matthew 13 verse 6, Luke 11 verse 28 and John 20 verse 29, you will find some 'blessed are you' moments.

The beatitudes are the sayings Jesus uses when he describes the people who are blessed by God. They include those on the margins of life, the poor, the grieving, the rejected, the oppressed, those desperate for justice. Many people that were thought to be cursed by God in some way, their lives having fallen apart. Jesus shocks everyone by saying, 'God is with them in their trouble and suffering. Right here with them.' And he demonstrates this by living it out, spending time with these folks, being a merciful peacemaker himself.

At the start of chapter 11 of Matthew's blog, we come across an incident where Jesus's cousin John sends some mates to Jesus to check him out, because John is worried that Jesus doesn't look much like the Messiah. It's a serious business for John because he's ended up in prison for speaking up for Jesus and the kingdom of God.

John's idea of the Messiah was of a kind of terminator God, a gladiator kind of deliverer, Russell Crowe crossed with Arnold Schwarzenegger. He imagined a Jesus that looks a little like Maximus Decimus Meridius, a leader who becomes a musclebound slave and then frees the people from the clutches of an evil empire.

But this isn't Jesus. He is very different. He looks more like Tom Hanks than Terminator Arnie. He's spending his time telling funny stories and hanging around with children, widows, prostitutes, fishermen and yes – the Romans that everyone hates. He doesn't look right at all. So John sends his friends to find out what's going on. John's having a crisis of faith – has he got it all wrong, has he picked the wrong guy?

Jesus's reply is simple. 'Open your eyes,' he says, 'look at what's happening around me. The blind start to see, the lame start to walk, people with leprosy are cured, the deaf can hear, the dead are coming back to life, and the Good News is being preached to the poor.' Jesus is fulfilling the beatitudes that he described when he started out.

And then he adds another beatitude, a coded message for John.
'Blessed are those who are not offended by me.' In other words, 'Blessed are those who are not fixed in their expectations about God, blessed are those who are not stuck in their ways. Blessed are those who can cope when God breaks out of the boxes they put him in.'

John had his ideas about Jesus.
'God is coming!' he had yelled, 'And you'll know it because he'll baptise with fire! He'll burn all that is rubbish, and he'll hack down all that's evil with his divine axe! Repent!'

Jesus turned out to be a little different.

We all have our own ideas about Jesus, and he will always break out of them. Are we ready for that? To have him smash the boxes we frequently put him in?

A Little Memento

Memento is an unusual film, a story told backwards about a guy called Leonard who has short-term memory loss. The reason for telling it backwards is so that, like Leonard, we do not know what has just taken place. In order to keep track of things Leonard writes down the important details of his life all over his body.

I write on my hand all the time. I scribble down the things I mustn't forget. God does the same. He's scribbled our names on his hand so he won't forget us. We're that important. At times we think he's forgotten, but he hasn't. He's got tattoos. ‘See. I have written your name on my hands.’ Have a look at Isaiah chapter 49 verses 14–16 for more info on this.

We're complex, we're on his hand, and we're fearfully and wonderfully made. Psalm 139 is an incredible song about this, about the God who understands us and is always with us, ever thinking about us. Not always easy for us to remember. Not always easy to believe. We look around and cannot see it. The media and those we know may well tell us otherwise. And feeling crap about ourselves is a common problem.

But that's why the writers of the Bible bash on and on about God being a compassionate creator. ‘Cause we need to hear it repeatedly, and we need things in our lives that will remind us. Because the systems of this world will tell us other things. They will tell us that meaning comes in a can. Or in the right look. The Bible celebrates people made in the image of God. Whatever their age, shape or condition. You could write that on your hand. Isaiah 44 verse 5 says: 'Some will write the Lord’s name on their hands...'

Flares, Capris and Eagles

Having grown up in the 1970s and now reached that age when 'so much was so much better back then' (the music, the TV, the flared trousers, the Ford Capris, Radio 1, the Battenberg cake... actually the Battenberg is still the same). Feel free to yawn by the way.

Anyway, being of that persuasion one of my highlights each weekend is listening to Johnny Walker and *Sounds of the Seventies* on Sunday, Radio 2 at 3pm. I remember listening to JW on Radio 1 in the 70s (did I mention how things were so much better back then?). Each week on his show now JW picks a classic album from that decade and this week he chose *Hotel California* by The Eagles.

This was one of the albums I bought and loved but then got very nervous about when I became a Christian. You see, the word on believer-street was that the title track *Hotel California* was very dodgy and had something to do with a Satanist High Temple. I think I burnt the album or smashed it up.

So I was extremely grateful when Johnny Walker explained what *Hotel California* was really about – the hedonistic lifestyle, the excesses and indulgence that The Eagles encountered in their rock'n'roll world and really knew an awful lot about.

The last track Johnny played from the album was one I had loved but forgotten about, it's called *The Last Resort* and if you have seven minutes (yes, seven minutes) to spare, feel free to go to YouTube and get your listening gear round this epic.

It's about (I think) those who took the land and abused it, though I am guessing. Back in the dark ages I just loved the sound and the poetry of it. When I first found the track on YouTube there was a perceptive and rather thought-provoking comment underneath it about the important difference between what we say and whether we actually do anything about it. And it brought me up short, because of course I am always sending out messages using songs, movies, TV, adverts and writing. And I have to put my hands up and say, 'You got me. It's a fair cop – I bash on about justice and kindness and the things that I believe matter to God, and yet I'm rampantly poverty-stricken when it comes to living that dream.'

I used to bash on about how we Christians needed to convert the world –- but I never converted many people, maybe one or two if I'm fortunate. Now I wax lyrical about caring for others, but my acts of compassion stand small in the grand scheme of things. It's easier to write and talk isn't it, than to knuckle down and get on with stuff. The world is full of unsung heroes, those we never hear about, who are quietly getting on with things, actually doing the stuff people like me talk about.

Jesus understands that. He once told a story about two sons, one of them was all talk and promised to help his old man. In the end he did nothing. The other refused to help his dad, then changed his mind and went and got his hands dirty. I hope I can occasionally change my mind and help my dad.

I pin my hopes on something Shane Claiborne once wrote:
'Get ready because God is preparing you for something very, very... small. Because it's small things that change the world.'

Reservoir God

A few years ago, whilst I was at Lee Abbey enjoying their Wayfarer's Arts Conference, I went along to a writing workshop by Richard Everett. He happened to comment on how the resurrection is a bit odd because there are no witnesses to it, even though it's the great climax of the story of Jesus. Richard said that it would be like making a heist movie and not showing the heist. At which point I piped up and said, 'Just like *Reservoir Dogs*!'

Reservoir Dogs is unusual because it's a film about a robbery, but we never see the crime. It's about the aftermath. And so is much of the New Testament – from the blog of Acts through to the multi-layered, big screen epic of Revelation. The heist we don't see, the resurrection with no witnesses.

At times people have gone looking for proof of the resurrection, and in their search some have become Christians. But it has to be said, Jesus himself did not stage it so that there was plenty of proof. The first witnesses to his miraculous return were women – hopeless and unreliable in a court of law. Sorry to be sexist here – but that's how it was in their culture. A woman's testimony did not stand up.

Christmas is different, that seems very carefully stage-managed so that certain people definitely get it. Mary's ancient cousin gets pregnant and becomes a surrogate mother to Mary for her first months in pregnancy. When Mary's baby arrives so do a bunch of shepherds. These are the comedy characters of the piece, the blonds of Jesus's day. Sometime after that several wise men roll up, who have rather dodgy theology and spend a lot of the time reading the stars. A couple of shuffling, wide-eyed saints later rattle over in the Jerusalem temple to see the new baby, and of course there are more angels flying about than you can shake a glitzy halo at.

Not so with Easter. Richard described it as 'a shy private affair between a grieving father and a dead son.'
Staged while the guards are asleep and no one is looking.
Someone else at the conference described a recent conversation with a friend who is an atheist, in which he had said, ' I admire your faith, I don't have enough faith to believe in atheism.' And that made me think we could come up with a new religion and call it – Faitheism. But I digress. Blatantly.

It seems to me that following Jesus is not about proving anything. Not really. If it is, the gospels are a bit of a mess. Why four? And why do they not all carry the same stories and agree on every single detail? And why is the resurrection told four different ways, a shambolic affair where people are running to and fro from the tomb, bumping into angels, soldiers and each other along the way. Perhaps this is because they aren't here to prove that Christianity is real or relevant, but instead they offer us their stories of encounters with Jesus in a chaotic world, inviting us to look closer; providing an opportunity for us to get to know God better.

When Jesus strolled out of a cracked tomb there was no huge crowd waiting and he didn't deliver a ground-breaking speech. Instead he quietly picked up a hoe and began working with his creation, waiting for the next passer-by to stop, look a little closer, ask questions and stumble upon the incredible truth.

He's Just a Fella

Just this week I watched a clip from that great old movie *Whistle Down the Wind*, and it reminded me of something. I saw this movie in the cinema, some time in the early 70s I think; it was made in 1961 but back then popular films did the cinema circuit for quite a while.

Hayley Mills has found a stranger in the barn and she thinks he is Jesus. Word goes around amongst the local children, but no one tells the adults. The scene I saw was the moment when everything falls apart in the story. It's little Charles's birthday party and, distracted by all the excitement, his sister Nan asks for an extra piece of cake. When asked why, she says that it's for Jesus. Oh oh – trouble. Nan's face falls. The truth has come out. The children's dreams are dashed. Little Charles, disappointed after the man in the barn did not look after his kitten, says, 'He's not Jesus, he's just a fella.'

This moment defines for me all those moments in cinema and life where you just hope it'll be all right but quite clearly it's fallen apart. Yet again. I get the same feeling whenever I watch *The Great Escape* and Steve McQueen hurls himself and his bike at the wire fence between him and Switzerland – maybe this time it'll be all right. Oh! No it won't. Drat. Poor Steve ends up tangled in spikes and captured once more.

But back to Charles and Nan and Hayley. Jesus said that it's really important to be like children in some ways. I don't think he meant it's good to be childish, but kids just say things out, don't they? They don't dress it up. And they have a great imagination and sense of wonder about things. They're curious and funny. And they have no secular-sacred divide. They don't put on holy voices to talk about God. My daughter can talk about Jesus one moment and Scooby Doo the next. It's all part of life to her. I like that. I like that a lot. I don't think God wants the holy voices and the shiny faces and the best outfits. He'd rather have the real people. The ones he made. The way children often are. I recall my dad being amazed when, as a young boy, I quite happily went up to a bishop after a confirmation service and asked straight out if I could be in a photograph with him. No airs or graces or worries. Just straightforward.

A couple of years ago we all enjoyed the British comedy *What We Did On Our Holidays*, made by the team who made BBC's *Outnumbered*. One of their tricks is to encourage the child actors to adlib, to make the most of the natural humour, honesty and curiosity of the children. The youngsters of course ask all the wrong questions, constantly wrong-footing and unmasking the adults. Something Jesus was a past-master at too. He longed to bring people into reality, apparently Jesus's phrase 'The truth will set you free', can also be translated 'Reality will set your free'. Jesus believed in that.

In the end in *Whistle Down the Wind* it turns out the man in the barn really is 'just a fella'. But as a parable the film is fascinating. When Charles asks the man in the barn about his sick kitten, he stands looking up towards the man's elevated hiding place, as if he is sending his pleas to the heavens. As the man is arrested there is a long shot of him being searched, standing in a crucified position; and as the police take him away his followers, a huge group of local children, come running to see. They are a real mixed bunch, some more committed than others. But they all come to see.

Children and Jesus. A powerful combination.

Not Very Christian

I have this photo next to my desk – a picture of a woman leaning over a gagged and blindfolded man from behind, armed with a pair of scissors. It's a black and white shot and at first glance looks rather ominous. A guy is bound and blind and a woman is coming at him with sharp scissors. Oh oh... but it's not what it seems. Close inspection reveals that she has come to cut him loose, to set him free. She's not come to do him damage but to rescue him. It's a dark image... about hope.

This was a lesson I learnt years ago, partly through this picture – that good news doesn't have to look nice and shiny. It can look dark and dangerous, mysterious and yes – often not very 'christian' or 'spiritual' at all. Jeremiah goes for the downright coarse approach in chapter two of his biblical blog. It's a good way of getting everyone's attention. Here's a bit of it retold in my book *Pulp Gospel*:

'Israel what happened to you? What happened?' Jeremiah yells, his voice bigger than him.
The people wait, Jeremiah will tell them, he always does.
'You used to be in love. You waited for your man to come to you, and then he swept you off your feet. He built a new home for you in a new land and bought you everything you could want. He set up home with you and gave you a new life. What did you do?'
They wait, Jeremiah will tell them.
'You turned into camels on heat!'
They laugh. Long and hard. He never fails to deliver a killer line.

'You weren't content with the good things in life, you wanted the bad things too. You were gagging for more, you sniffed the breeze and turned into donkeys.'
More laughter.
'Listen to you – braying like asses!'
They don't like that one so much.
'You are like dumb, stubborn mules, making love to anything that you can find. Camels and jackasses. You'll have anything. You once had beauty and wealth and dignity and you've traded it all so you can romp about the desert looking for someone to satisfy you. You're ugly and sweating and dirty.'

The big mistake we can make when communicating about God is thinking that we must always make it sound and look nice, tidy, neat and 'christian'. Yet goodness can be delivered in all kinds of ways.

Bishop Nick Baines has a saying I like, he tells his new curates: 'I don't mind heresy, just don't bore me.' I like that. I don't want to be so concerned about getting the good news 'right' that I make it boring, and lose all the laughter and mystery and danger of it.

In many of the dark comic book films that are around these days the struggle is still the same – the battle of good versus evil. Many of these films don't look very nice though. *The Matrix* was a hugely popular film at the end of the 1990s, it was gloomy and grim, yet was a story about breaking free from the shackles of this world. Teenagers loved it.

We don't need to compromise when offering tales of good news, but we don't need to make them technicolour either. Sometimes it's a picture of a woman approaching a bound man with a pair of scissors.

Dave, Quentin, Paul and Jesus

When I first went on Twitter I followed three people – comedian Dave Gorman, film maker Quentin Tarantino and all round jolly egg Stephen Fry. This meant that when I visited Twitter comments from these three came up interspersed with each other, and it looked for all the world like they were having a totally deranged chat. Stephen would comment on Japan and Dave would then say how it's square and covered in polyurethane and then Quentin would mention that it has a couple of shotguns and a dancer with a snake round her neck. You couldn't make it up could you?

Actually you could because I did, but their real conversations were similar to that, looking as if they were answering the questions no one was asking.

I'm not very good at tweeting to be honest. I'm a Twitter pimp, a social network mercenary just using it for my own ends. I tend to use it to advertise my work. But a while ago my sister-in-law opened my eyes to the power of social media when she described a conference she had just attended where the delegates were encouraged to tweet as the speakers delivered from the stage. This created all kinds of live debate and feedback which was of course visible not just to those at the conference, but anyone in the known world. And as often happens with things like this my mind turned immediately to church and how we do it on a Sunday.

What would happen if we could tweet each other during the service? Reacting, debating, arguing, passing comments to each other. Bearing in mind that the whole world might be watching. Who knows what might happen? Who might just stumble across the good news by coming across our Sunday

Service Tweeting? The minister says something and we can then react in front of a global audience. What do you think?

You know two people who I'm sure would agree?

Paul and Jesus.

In fact I'm sure they'd encourage it. Debate, questions and argument were a vital part of first century learning, so tweeting has surely provided the ideal tool for us to get back to a much more biblical style of teaching. My sister-in-law told me that one of the reasons they encourage tweeting in conferences is this: we need to lose control of our content in order for it to influence others. We have to set it free.

Now that's frightening for many of us Christians because we worry that people must have the right theology. But Jesus was more relaxed than that.

He asked people what they thought of his stories, inviting debate and comeback. And he told the tale of the bad farmer who wasn't very accurate when he sowed his crop, not sowing seed in just good soil, but in the rocks and thistles and even on the path where people walk. A daft and wasteful way to sow crops. But that's what Jesus did, sent out his message and lost control of it, confident that God's word would not return empty. He told his stories and let them go viral.

Dare we? Dare I?

The Fruitcake Bible

The Bible's not easy to read is it? I mean, okay, a lot of Christians read bits of Paul's letters and a few stories from the gospels. But Lamentations? Deuteronomy? Ecclesiastes? Leviticus?
And many of us focus on just a few of the things Jesus did.

The Bible is certainly jam-packed with incredible stories but that can be the problem – it's this that makes it so very dense, and the good bits have ended up crammed tightly together in there. A bit like a fruitcake. In fact, if the Bible was a fruitcake it would be so dense you couldn't slice through it. You'd need a chainsaw, and you'd have to wear a helmet and goggles to protect yourself from the millions of shards and splinters that might hit you in the face when you opened it up. (Mind you, there may be times when reading the Bible is maybe supposed to feel like you've been hit in the face with a handful of sharp splinters.)

If you're like me you need other people to hack it apart for you. Professional Bible chefs (or surgeons, to mix my metaphors) who know what they're doing.

When introducing the Bible I have often used a clip from the beginning of the movie *A Series of Unfortunate Events*. A happy little elf comes bouncing onto the screen and jolly music plays in the background. Then there is the sound of a needle scraping on a record and the elf freezes in mid hop while the music stops abruptly. Then the voiceover says something like, 'This is not a film about a happy little elf, if you want a film like that go to screen two. However, if you like stories about spies, leeches and secret organisations, then stay.'

This is what has happened to me regarding the Bible. For years I thought it was a happy book containing all the nice shiny people and the nice shiny answers. Like a Disney movie. When my life fell apart and I was anything but nice and shiny I needed another kind of book. And that's when I discovered that the Bible had been that book all along – a very different kind of read indeed. I began to learn about characters who struggled with life and wrestled with God; the prophets who used humour and sarcasm and irony to communicate; the disciples, in the Old and New Testament, who frequently wanted to resign as followers of God. In short, I found that it wasn't the adventures of the happy little elf, but a tale of dark doings, and inappropriate people.

If you've read some of my other blog posts you may have encountered my references to the BBC series of *Horrible Histories*. This has inspired me no end, not least because my daughter now loves learning history as a result of it. A while ago she put a certain amount of effort into learning the words to a comedy song which taught her the names of all the kings and queens of England. When my wife and I chatted about this, Lynn said to me, 'At school it's all about memorising dates – and that overlooks a lot of the interesting stories.'

That's what I think about the Bible. We often place emphasis on learning little quotes and reciting bite-sized chunks without understanding the people and stories behind and within them. These stories bring the Bible to life and create genuine connections for us. I believe, with a little help, anyone can find themselves in the good book. Anyone. Whatever we believe. But we have to find ways to break open this fruitcake, to see the whole thing differently. To quote a line from the movie *Patch Adams*, 'You have to see what no one else sees. See what everyone else chooses not to see.' Jesus did that. He saw things very differently. He took the Hebrew Bible (the Old Testament) and retold it using prostitutes and children, corrupt judges and good wine.

I heard a while back that Richard Dawkins made a comment about how the church has had control of the Bible for too long. I'm with Richard here, I'm all for that. I think we need to de-churchify the Bible – and get it onto the streets and in the brothels and cinemas and toilets and supermarkets and sports stadiums and anywhere really. Anywhere where this earthy book full of life makes sense. But I guess that takes work, and to do that I need to read it differently, see it differently, tell it differently. And not be frightened to do what the writers of the gospels did – to tell it in ordinary contemporary language.

It's often forgotten that the biblical blogs of Matthew, Mark, Luke and John were not written in a holy, special language, but in the street language of their day. Perhaps we need to seriously consider de-christianising our language. Ouch! That's hard, when you've spoken christianese for years it's very difficult to speak about your faith in other ways. How might we do that?

I think I've digressed a little here - so to drag myself back to my original point. When I open the Bible I find a God who met crooks, losers, rebels and reluctant disciples and saw them differently. Let's not miss out on their stories, because their stories are most likely our stories too.

I'll finish with a couple of lines, one from a song by singer Sheryl Crowe, the other from the biblical blog of Ecclesiastes – a strange book full of difficult questions. (But then, most of us are strange people full of difficult questions.) Ecclesiastes is a book written by someone who has all they could ask for, and yet they're still unhappy. ‘Everything is meaningless,’ says the teacher, ‘Everything is so weary and tiresome! No matter how much we see, we are never satisfied. No matter how much we hear, we are not content.’ Now there's a perfect book for us in the relatively affluent yet dissatisfied West. We have sex, money, food, drink... and we still want more. We are not content.

Sheryl Crowe once sang about the same kind of thing, and so I’ll finish with her lines.
'If it makes you happy then it can't be that bad,
If it makes you happy then why are you still so sad?'
See what I mean?

I admit that this chapter has meandered, but then so does the Bible sometimes and so do we. Hope there’s something useful in this unruly torrent of words.

No Plan B

In a scene from the film *Kingdom of Heaven* Balion is a few knights short of an army. In fact -- he has no knights at all. He is trapped in the city of Jerusalem and the place is surrounded. Yikes! What are they gonna do? I know -- brilliant idea – let's take a load of people without the proper experience or training and turn them into knights. That'll work. Genius idea! I love this scene from *Kingdom of Heaven*. Oddly enough it always makes me think of The Day of Pentecost, which turns up in June each year, fifty days after Easter. Nowadays we sometimes call it the birthday of the church, but that sounds to me a little too much like children's TV. The DOP (as we shall now refer to it) is a lot more adult than that if you ask me.

I particularly enjoy the moment in this scene when Balion slaps one of the newly appointed knights across the face so they won't forget their commission. Maybe we should do that when people join the church. Enough of the hugging and the free cups of tea. A broken nose, that'll remind you of the importance of what we're doing here. (Only kidding.)

What Balion does in this clip is not a million miles away from the events on the DOP. God takes a whole load of people who haven't had the right training or experience and commissions them to be his people. They haven't been on an Alpha course or read anything by Rick Warren or John Ortberg and yet here they are being given the responsibility of changing the planet. So, er... what's your Plan B, God?

What? Oh. Really? No Plan B? None at all? Rrrrrrrrrrrrright. Are you sure? I mean, I wouldn't pick me, if I were you. I'm not always reliable. I have mood swings. And I don't really fit in. Plus, when I do try and do a job I'm a bit of a control freak. I want things done my way. When I'm organising something I know how I want it to go and I do my best to steer things in that direction. Sometimes driving myself and others mad along the way. The verse 'We can make our plans but God has the last word' from the book of Proverbs has always made me smile.

Well, the DOP shows me that God is most definitely not a control freak. I mean, why would you pick that bunch of people? They won't necessarily do it right. Some of them will misuse the power, some of them abuse it. Some use it for monetary gain, some of us will start and then give up half-way. None of us will really understand it.

'Well,' says God, 'you know, I think I'll take a chance on it. See how it goes, see what happens. I like a challenge. And I want people to be involved.'

When the Israelites came to Mount Sinai after getting out of Egypt, Moses promised them that God was going to make them into a kingdom of priests, a holy nation. In other words, his reps on earth. Bit of a shock when they had come from a society where only certain people were allowed to operate as priests. Even today it's a bit of a shock – we tend to come from cultures where you have to be chosen and ordained and trained to be a priest. But no, in one of his emails in the good book Peter reminds the followers that Moses's commission still stands.

'You are a chosen people,' he writes. 'You are a kingdom of priests, God's holy nation...'

The same commission – God's image on the earth gets the job of being God's representatives on earth.

'Be brave... speak the truth... safeguard the helpless...' to quote Balion.
Yikes.
The DOP seems to me to be a reboot of that original promise.

'There you go,' says God, 'I said I'd do it. Here are the tools you'll need. You can learn on the job. Make a few mistakes (in fact, make a lot of mistakes) and be better for it. Go on... Give it a try. You're my chosen people, you're my priests. You can all be my CEOs on the earth. Off you go... go on... that includes you at the back there, Hopwood... stop messing about and join in...'

Lady Madonna

A few years ago Lady Gaga released a song called *Judas* – a good friend sent me the lyrics – quite an interesting mash up of Easter bits and pieces. I'm not sure it says much about Lady Gaga but it did remind me of Madonna and her *Like a Prayer* song and video. Lady Gaga does remind me of Madonna – both outrageous and talented performers, doing everything to grab an audience. And sounding like each other sometimes. Madonna hasn't yet worn a meat dress, but she'll probably come up with a skunk skirt before too long.

Years ago I watched a documentary which asked the question – Can you laugh at religion? It opened my eyes to the fact that for most comedians religion is just another subject matter. We may get nervy and upset when we see and hear jokes (and indeed pop videos and songs) about what we believe and hold as precious, but these things are not necessarily personal attacks on our faith. Singing about Judas or Prayer is another way that powerful pop divas can get your attention.

Lady Gaga's song made me think it might be worth writing a story about a woman in love with Judas. Thinking about him from the angle of someone who loved him, now that would be a whole other story. It's so easy to make the biblical characters two-dimensional – cast members just playing a part so that Jesus can do his stuff. But let's face it – Judas had a mum and dad, a favourite food, a childhood, and teenage angst. He had his fears and his hopes and his history.
Maybe even sex appeal, though I doubt it was much like Lady Gaga's portrayal in her song.

One thing that stands out is the difference between the U.S. and the U.K. when it comes to religious stuff. I doubt if most of the kids in the U.K. will understand the references in Madonna's or Lady Gaga's songs. When the film *Bruce Almighty* came out I think lots of people in the UK didn't get it. Unlike those stateside who are still a lot more clued in when it comes to Christianity. This could make songs like these into useful tools. If you're listening closely it may throw up all the right questions. I mean – what's Lady Gaga going on about? Why does she mention washing feet with hair? Why betrayal? And why three times? Why the reference to kings and crowns?

I leave the questions with you.

Feel free to discuss.
Or not.

What Song Would You Sing?

A few years ago I spent time working on a book about pop music and the psalms and the kind of songs that have changed my life. There is a scene I like in the film *Walk the Line*, the story of Johnny Cash. At this point in the movie the young Mr Cash is desperate to get a recording contract so he rolls up at a small local recording studio to cut a single. However things don't go according to plan. The gospel song he and his band roll out does not impress the producer at all. He claims he can't market gospel like that anymore. When Johnny asks what's wrong with the song, the producer tells him he doesn't believe him. This angers Johnny who wants to know more. So the producer asks Johnny, if he was lying in the gutter with just time left to sing one song before he died, what would he choose? Would he choose this old gospel number that is always playing on the radio? Or would he choose something else? Something that is real for him? Because, the producer says, it's that kind of reality that truly saves people. Not just trotting out well-worn songs for the sake of it.

Songs are a massive part of my life, I'm one of those annoying people who, on hearing a quote from something, will then break out into a tuneless version of a song featuring that line. For five years as a teenager I meticulously kept a record of the music charts in a series of notebooks. I knew all the movers and shakers, climbers and fallers in the current Top 30, as it was then, later to become the Top 40.

Songs take me back to certain times in my life, I can often date events by recalling the songs that were around at that time and when they were in the charts. I'm full of useful musical facts. I can tell you that The Who have never had a number one single and The Rolling Stones have had five. Take That have never had a Christmas number one whereas the Spice Girls had three in a row. The only other band to have three Christmas number ones in a row were The Beatles. See? It's all vital information isn't it?

Anyway, with this scene about Johnny Cash in mind I was wondering what song you might choose, if you had to. Are there songs that will always mean something to you? Songs you heard or sang at certain times in your life. I've come to the conclusion that most music has the potential to be spiritual. Not just Christian music, all music.

When I became a Christian I stopped listening to ordinary chart music, and in fact got rid of all my albums. For 6 years I only listened to Christian music. But I never stopped loving pop music and in 1988 I started buying it again. Taking a break from it helped change my attitude towards it, I had in an odd way been addicted to it. Sounds dramatic, but I had just got into the habit of buying a lot of it and not necessarily listening to it.

Now I listen all over again, thanks to YouTube, Spotify, mp3s and the good ol' radio. And like movies, songs often make me think about my faith and God's place in the world. I really like something Jesus said about knowing the truth and then the truth setting us free. Seems to me that pop songs are loaded with truth. Not necessarily happy truth, or liberating truth, often they are commenting on the emptiness of life, or the pain in the world, or the confusion and heartache in so many people. But truth all the same, and truth can open doors.

So how about you? Any meaningful melodies kicking around out there? Anything that gets you through the day, lights your fire, floats your boat, toasts your bread, boils your kettle, fries your egg or boots your laptop? (I think you get the picture.)

When challenged about the song he would sing, Johnny Cash replies with a song he has written about a man in prison who has shot someone. And the producer can see the reality and power in it. Later on Johnny would go on to receive piles of mail from prisoners touched by his music and as a result he started to play live concerts in various prisons.

So, what song would you sing?

It's True! I Am a Fraud!!

It always used to make me smile when I typed my name into YouTube, because listed there was a video entitled 'Dave Hopwood pissed as a fart'. When I first saw it I got a sudden feeling of panic wondering if it was in fact me, exposed to the world having had too many beers. Also, apparently, I was 'a fag in 6th grade'. Shocking stuff eh!!
I don't think those terrible misdemeanours are there now. (Although I can confirm – that particular Dave Hopwood mentioned in those videos did not prove to be me.)

One of the things I am increasingly aware of is my total lack of ability to be a good person. And it's not only me. I've had many conversations with people who are extremely aware of their failures, and their lack of ability to be a better Christian. And many of us are often preoccupied and troubled by this problem.

It has made me consider, again and again, this question. Is being a Christian really about trying to be a perfect, better or good person? The verdict? I don't think so. And I think that we can misunderstand Jesus on the point. It's sometimes quoted that he said, 'Be perfect as your heavenly father is perfect.' (Matthew 5 v 48)
Well sure he did, but context is everything here. He was talking to religious leaders who believed they were good people, and Jesus jokingly pulled them up on the point and said, effectively,
'You think you're good? Well, shape up, to play that game you have to be really good, I mean really **really** good, you know – perfect! Can you do that?'
And he knew they would never manage it. So he hoped to make them think again and consider what to do about their

lack of perfection. You see, he didn't invite us to be better people, he invited us to follow.

And I have concluded this. Following Jesus is not so much about stopping being bad, I think it's more about understanding what he did and following the same way.

In his book *The Orthodox Heretic* Pete Rollins tells a story (called The Payoff) of an old priest who is victimised by a young prince. The prince hates him and imprisons some of his congregation. But the priest refuses to give up his work. So one day the prince gets a load of money together, goes to see him and says this.
'For 10,000 rupees I want you to write a letter to everyone around here admitting you are a fraud and a fake and not a good Christian at all.'
The priest thinks about this for a while and then says, 'All right. I'll write to everyone and admit that. But on three conditions. One, you must stop victimising my congregation, two, you must set free those in prison, and three... you'll need to give me a few days to get the money together, 10,000 rupees is a lot of money, and I'm a poor man.'

In his conclusion about this story Pete says this.
'...people of faith will not only have a profound understanding of their own weaknesses but also freely acknowledge them.'

I think Paul a.k.a 'the Saint' would have concurred.
In fact he did. In chapter 7 of his email to the Romans he wrote this:
'I know I am rotten through and through so far as my old sinful nature is concerned. No matter which way I turn, I can't make myself do right. I want to, but I can't. When I

want to do good, I don't. And when I try not to do wrong, I do it anyway.'

This is astonishing writing really, Paul is coming clean, admitting his struggles with life. What is his conclusion? Well, the ongoing help of Jesus. No surprise there really.
'Who will free me from my sin-dominated life,' he writes, 'thank God, Jesus can.' But he is not done yet with the bad news, he then writes, 'In my mind I want to obey God's law, but because of my flawed nature I am a slave to sin.'

The chapter ends there, but originally there was no break, this just flowed into the next line, 'There is now no condemnation for those who belong to Jesus.' So it seems Paul continues his battle but says that the way forward is with Jesus. He knows his frailty, but knows too that the solution is to keep pressing on with Jesus. Following his way in spite of our limps and stumbling weakness.

You're Gonna Need a Bigger Cake

When Kate and Will got married I watched a few of the scenes on YouTube. Not exactly a quiet wedding was it?
The best bit for me was... I'm sorry, not the dress... I mean... like – a dress is a dress, isn't it?

The best bit was seeing all those people in the streets moving together towards the palace. All those people forgetting their troubles and celebrating because something better was happening. Something that scooped them up and carried them into a new place, a new day. The sense of celebration and lack of cynicism was astonishing. And as I watched, it started me thinking about the wedding that the writers of the Bible describe. (Check out Isaiah's blog chapter 65 verse 17, somewhere around page 604 if you own my Bible, or try Revelation chapter 21, at the back of the Good Book.) The wedding between God and the people.

And I realised something afresh – it's not about some little service somewhere with a few family and friends, or even a big service somewhere attended by thousands. This is about good news that changes our lives, breaks us out of the old ways and takes us into something new. As played out by those crowds of extras, moving towards the palace.

This Kate and Will bash is what the anarchists would call a TAZ – a temporary autonomous zone -- an event which is temporary and unusual and which brings down the barriers between people (Kester Brewin writes about this in his book *Other*). Like the days when it snows. People are different towards each other. You could say communities like Lee Abbey in Devon and Scargill House in Yorkshire create one of these every week – a different place where, for a short time, you can be more vulnerable. It only works because the experience for a visiting guest is temporary.

However you celebrated Kate and Will’s bash – and I was tempted to just go back to bed -- there's no denying the good news of this biblical wedding picture. Jesus the bridegroom, throwing the biggest wedding in the world, an event to which everyone is invited. When most of those people who camped out in London in order to be a part of things look back, I bet they won't just remember the dress, or the double kiss on the balcony, I'll bet they'll think on the whole experience. The new society that was formed just for a day.

The new community of followers who came to the future king's wedding.

How Did It Come to This?

I very recently attended a service where panic broke loose. All was going well – i.e. controlled, reverent and peaceful – then it came to the time to take the bread and wine, an act which involved queuing up at the front of the church.

Oh oh.

One young boy refused to get up and take it. Nope. No siree. No dice. Wouldn't play ball.

No amount of coaxing or cajoling from the adults around him would make him budge. It was like he refused to eat his greens or something. Now I admit, it was only a mildly panic-stricken moment, the service continued and most people hardly noticed. But I did.

I like it when our services go wrong sometimes. When God punches out of our cardboard boxes.

And it made me wonder... how did following Jesus come to this? Why are our gatherings so carefully controlled and orchestrated? Do they need to be? I mean let's face it, when Jesus was walking around nobody had the faintest idea what was going to happen next. And even when he went along to ordered events – e.g. the synagogue and temple meetings, the Passover meal, three funerals and a wedding – he put his foot in it and messed things up completely. Perhaps that had something to do with the man who embodied life in all its fullness, as opposed to operating within neat lines of predictability. It may well be true that some churches come to life when the service is done and they crack out the coffee and the biscuits. Or doughnuts if you're lucky. Adrian Plass once commented on this phenomenon, saying that poor old God must look down and think – 'That's not fair! My bit was all cold and organised and 'orrible, your bit's all happy and fun and interesting...' I think Adrian said something like that anyway.

The service I was attending that day was a kind of all-age event, without most of the all-age bit. This really isn't intended as a criticism, it's a small country church and the number of kids they had gathered was impressive in itself; but much of the service must have been incomprehensible to most of them, and perhaps to a few of the adults present too. We sang songs with all kind of complex theological imagery strung together in quick succession. Not much of it connecting with daily life in a small rural community.

Unlike Jesus who was very good at connecting with life in his small rural community.

Nick Page's book *The Longest Week* is a detailed analysis of life in the last week leading up to Jesus's death. And a thumping good read it is too. My head was spinning after reading it. Towards the end he comments on a certain strange occurrence at the first Easter.

One of the stories we often read in the Bible around this time is that the curtain in the Temple in Jerusalem was mysteriously torn in two when Jesus died. Now the traditional symbolic view is that this means we now have access to God, because of Jesus's death. But there's a second view, one I like very much. The temple curtain is torn, not so much to provide an entrance – but as an exit. God's escaped! He's on the loose, he's fled the temple and he's out in the streets and the pubs and the betting shops and the sports stadiums. He's on the Internet and the TV. On the iPhones and the e-readers. No stopping him now. Can't contain him in the religious buildings anymore. Jesus has done something and God has broken loose from our organised moorings. He’s out there. Don't miss him whatever you do.

He's Not the Messiah... He's a Very...

I've had a couple of experiences of Easter this week. I took a mind-bending photo of myself and two friends in the cinema where we went to see the film *Hop*. It was the gripping tale of the Easter Bunny, no doubt based on true accounts.

The picture I took messes with your perception, because it's me taking a picture of me, but from a long way off, due to the mirrors on the high ceiling of the cinema foyer. I just pointed my phone upwards and clicked. In the shot I'm very small and holding a phone, taking a picture of myself holding a phone, taking a picture of myself holding a phone etc. As I say, it messes with my head a bit. And I mention it because I think Easter should mess with our heads a bit. There's nothing that frustrates me more than just telling the same old story the same old way – especially on Easter Sunday morning when we all roll up to church and are expected to suddenly be ecstatic that Jesus has risen from the dead, even though we already knew that when we ate our *Weetabix* that morning. (Other Easter morning breakfasts are available.)

The hapless bunch on the first Easter Sunday were scared, confused, angry, disappointed and emotionally wrung out. Their experience of that Sunday was a very different affair. They had no idea what was going on, if they should be fearful or hopeful. Various people claimed to have seen Jesus or if not him, the empty tomb he should have been in, but it would be a little while before the truth really crystallised. And even then a lot of powerful people would contest it. They had various fixed ideas about the Messiah and Jesus just wouldn't play along. No way. And he still won't. He continues to break out of our neat Christian boxes.

It seems to me that the more you look at Jesus the more you find he isn't the guy you thought he was. Which is often good news.

I have a photograph from an Easter presentation I was part of a couple of years ago at the Lee Abbey conference centre in Devon. It's a picture of Jesus, but it's shocking for a couple of reasons. Firstly he is made up to look bruised and beaten, and secondly he is being played by a woman. A good friend at the time, Claire. We had four different actors playing Jesus, at various points in the Easter story. I pinched the idea from a film about Bob Dylan called *I'm Not There*, in which six actors play the gravelly man at different times, including, yes – a woman. Cate Blanchett I believe.

At the point in the Easter story when Claire played Jesus I wanted to shake the audience, to get to the heart of what it must have felt like to have the Messiah appear, and look all wrong. At this moment he looked vulnerable, weak, and shocking; and like a failed criminal. To risk throwing in a darkly humorous line, we might at this point concur with a quote from *Life of Brian*,
'He's not the Messiah, he's a very naughty boy.'

Jesus spent many days looking like a very naughty boy, and never more so than when they brought him out, barely able to stand, looking weak and broken and bloodied. On trial for his life. A crooked loser.

Theologian and author Tom Wright says that on Good Friday we find the clash of two kingdoms – the might of the Roman empire meets the weakness of God head on. Which one is still with us 2000 years later?

A final Easter thought, inspired by Nick Page's book, *The Longest Week*.

Jerusalem streets were paved with... not gold... but filth. Most folks lived in relative poverty (think *Slumdog Millionaire*) and there were more open sewers than you could shake a loo brush at. That's why you got your feet washed. And not by just anybody, by a gentile slave. An unclean piece of low life. Jewish slaves were forbidden to do the job - only a gentile slave could handle that muck. Because they were unclean anyway. Oh! What's happening now? Jesus is doing an impersonation... of a crud-scraping, untouchable piece of scum. What's your response? Well... in the eloquent words of Peter, the rocky one,
'Errrr... what? Master, you... why? er... not my... oh no!!'
That was all he got out. He could not believe that this Messiah was doing the toilet cleaning job.

Theologian Tom Wright points out that this wasn't the first time Jesus washed feet. In many ways Jesus did this kind of thing every day, it characterised his life. Jesus regularly made himself look stupid, repellent, small. Offensive. Ugly. This was his way of changing the world.

Happy Easter. (For whenever it next comes along.)

The Wrong Question?

For years I have feared arriving at the Pearly Gates only to face *that* question – the one so many preachers like to talk about.
'Did you really believe in Jesus Christ?' (Similar alternatives include, 'Have you accepted Jesus Christ?' and 'Have you given your life to Jesus Christ?' This said, please note – it's not multiple choice.)

Before I saw myself as a fully-fledged believer I feared that I might have to say 'No' and would then be turned away. Condemned to an eternity in Toastville.
After I became a Christian I still feared that question – because maybe I wasn't *actually* a real Christian, even though I thought I was. Maybe I hadn't *really* repented enough, said the right words, prayed the right prayer, *really* asked Jesus into my life. Or maybe my theology just wasn't right? A fear that continues to rear its head from time to time.

Scene – the Pearly Gates.
Death: Did you believe in Jesus, Dave?
Me: Yes... er... I think so.
Death: Aha! Gotcha! No! You didn't -- you just *thought* you did. You didn't concentrate hard enough. Off you go to Toastville.

But lately I've been wondering. What if that's the wrong question?

I mean, what does it mean to believe in something anyway? Is it about saying the right prayer or stating the right phrase? Or something else?

If I say I believe chocolate is bad for you, but then eat a lot of it (guilty on that one) I'm surely lying when I say I believe it's bad for you. Because you live what you believe, don't you? And I don't live as if I believe chocolate is second only to arsenic. You see, I could say I believe that *Dragons' Den* is tosh – but then give away my true beliefs by watching it faithfully. I can say I believe in helping people. But not do much of it... I'm sure you get the picture. It seems to me we live what we believe. We can't help it.

St Paul, the evangelist formerly known as Saul, says we'll be saved if we state with our mouth and believe in our heart that Jesus is Lord. Well there you go... the heart is the seat of our being and doing. If I believe something in my heart then I live it, don't I? Don't I?? If I believe with my heart that Jesus is compassionate I'd better start living some of that. Start copying my rabbi. That's what disciples did. Peter certainly saw it that way.
'Why are you trying to walk on water, Pete?'
''Cause that's what my rabbi's up to – look!'

When he saw Jesus walking on water Peter had to have a go, to do what his rabbi was doing. Jesus himself said that he did what his father was doing. Jesus believed his father and that meant he copied his father.

These days, as I read the Bible, I find a Jesus who says things like, 'People will know you're a believer when they see you acting with love, in fact that's how the whole world will know you.' And also, 'A tree is identified by the kind of fruit it produces.' I find a Jesus who tells stories about people who demonstrate compassion i.e. The Sheep and the Goats story; and generosity i.e. The Rich Idiot story; and forgiveness i.e. The Unforgiving Servant. It's interesting to note in that

particular ripping yarn that the outcome of the servant being forgiven is that he will become more forgiving. He will act differently towards other people.
So now I fear another question. A second question.
And the post-daisy-pushing-up conversation might go something like this.

Scene – the Pearly Gates.
St P: So, er... Mr Hopgood...
Me: No, it's Hop*wood* actually.
St P: Really? Are you sure?
Me: Well I always I thought so. Seemed to work all right at school when they called the register...
St P: Right. Whatever. Well anyway, Mr Hopcroft, did you believe in Jesus?
Me: Yes.
St P: Really? Are you sure?
Me: Ye-e-e-s... Well, I always thought so... sort of. I tried to be absolutely sure. Grit my teeth, clench my fists. Say it loudly to myself that I'd been born again. Name it and claim it, you know all that sort of thing...
St P: Name it and what? Oh, never mind. Whatever. So (coming to the killer question) ... why didn't you live more like him then?
Me: What?!
St P: Jesus – if you believed in him – why didn't you live more like him?

Ouch!

And I'd have to put my hands up and say – yep, you got me there – bang to rights. I said I believed a lot of things about Jesus, I said I was following him, but if you look at my CV...

Good ol' St Paul was very aware of this snag. He grew more aware of it the older he got. My favourite St Paul email is what we now call Romans 7. I love it because the big man comes clean. I think I've mentioned this already, but only because I find it so helpful. It's worth quoting again.

'I can't do it,' he says, 'I say I believe in Jesus, but I don't live like him. I do things Jesus wouldn't do, and I don't do things he would do. I'm lost. I'll get to those gates and hang my head. I haven't lived what I believed. Where's the hope?'

But then, a week later, he sends his next email. And he's discovered something. Romans 8 starts with this.

'Thank God, there's a solution. Jesus takes care of the problem!'

In a sense the problem is also the solution. That's what they call grace.

Back to the Pearly Gates then.

St P: You didn't live much like Jesus then, Mr Hopweed? You know, being kind, compassionate, big-hearted, humble?

Me: Nope.

St P: In fact... looking at your CV – I'd give you 1 out of 10, and that's being generous.

Me: Yep.

St P: Still...

Me: (pouncing on a tiny modicum of hope here) Still what?

St P: Well... Jesus knew you'd be pretty rubbish at it. He knew you're believing capability was about the size of an amoeba's armpit... smaller in fact. So... you're off the hook. More than off the hook. You pass with flying colours. Get in here.

Me: What? But... I was terrible.

St P: Course you were... no – you were worse than terrible... you were cataclysmically bad, you were the Genghis Khan of the followers of Jesus... you were the Bin Laden of believers... if it was up to me you'd be roasting on a spit, garnished with garlic and onions in a white wine sauce. (sniffs) But lucky for you – I'm not God, and God doesn't think like me – or like you come to that. He thinks like Jesus. Which is just as well for you. 'Cause Jesus has sorted it. You are one lucky bad believer. Now get in and start partying. The punk rockers are first on the left.

That's how I hope the Pearly Gates scenario will pan out anyway.

Life at the Launderette

...would never be the same again. That groundbreaking *Heard It Through the Grapevine* advert for Levi jeans first went out in 1985 and the earth shivered on its axis as a result. Some people's lives really would never be the same. For a while anyway. Nick Kamen – the guy who removed his jeans and put the things in the washing machine – his life changed a bit. Plus I'm sure we all bought some jeans – but the thing that really happened, the thing that changed forever (or at least for a twinkle or two) was that, apparently, we all raided our dads' boxer shorts drawer. Or went out and bought some new trendy boxers as a result of the advert. Till then, boxers had been old and flabby. Now they were cool cool cool. Wear boxer shorts and women in launderettes will love ya.

This was the first time that music had played such a vital role in selling, and it's been doing the same ever since. When I was a whole lot younger I remember sending off for a couple of Levi's posters and putting them up on my bedroom wall. Even though I had probably never worn Levi's. Or undressed in front of a couple of washers. Mind you – that was way back in the dark days of the 1970s, probably before Nick Kamen was out of nappies. Levi nappies obviously.

One of my all-time favourite adverts is the one with the woman in the VW Beetle, who, broken-hearted, pulls up on a clifftop and makes her world feel better by brewing some instant coffee. If only life were so easy. Apparently sales of bottled water, VW Beetles, portable water-heater filaments and er... oh yea... a particular brand of coffee were all affected by it.

Advertising works I guess, and maybe that's what Jesus needs – a good advertising campaign. Perhaps he needs girls in cars, crying on clifftops, and guys washing their jeans in launderettes, then everyone would want him wouldn't they?

Wouldn't they?
Or would they?

He once, no twice, got the attention of the general public when he fed thousands of people with a packet of rolls and a couple of fish fingers. What you might call the first Flash Mob. That got his name about a bit. Shame there were no cameras or advertising executives around to capture the moment for him. He also then spoilt it by refusing any more Flash Mob miracles and he instead offered people a cold plate of reality. They didn't want that. No thanks. They wanted the easy street of magic bread, not the boot camp of genuine faith.

I doubt Jesus would have been interested in jeans or boxers or VW Betles to sell his product. He'd probably have ruined the advert by insisting on walking on the set saying things like – 'You can't follow me unless you're prepared to go to the electric chair first.' Along with an invitation to be more humble and look a little bit mad in the eyes of the majority.
Tricky that.
'Cut! Take 493! Jesus, can you please stay out of the shot? You're ruining your own advertising campaign.'

Jesus *was* big on straplines though.
He didn't say – 'Because you're worth it.' Or 'Concentrate, here's the science bit.' Or 'Keep calm and carry gum.' Or even 'It does exactly what it says on the tin.'
Phrases which now seem to be everywhere.

But he did have other catchphrases and straplines.
'I have come to bring you life in all its fullness.'
'You'll know the truth and the truth will set you free.'
And probably the most famous of them all.
'God so loved the world that he sent his only son, not to be its judge, but to be its saviour.'
And if you're having a bad day, he also said, 'In this world you'll have trouble, but be encouraged, I've overcome this harsh world.'

To sum up in one soundbite, what you might call The King's Speech, he said, 'Blessed are the poor, the meek, the persecuted, the peacemakers.'
You can check these straplines any time. In the gospels of Matthew, Mark, Luke and John. Or you can Google them for the specific Bible reference. Not easy to market them though. A half-naked man in a launderette is more appealing than a totally naked one stretched out like a piece of raw meat on a criminal's cross.

'Cut.'

How Did I Become a Dad?

All right, hold on a minute! I know what you're thinking... and before you all start emailing me with the biological shenanigans of it all, I do know how it happened on a birdy-bee-kind of level. But it's not a birds and bees issue I have in mind here.

When my oldest daughter was at junior school we lived in a little village, and for the first time in her life my daughter was able to walk to and from school. And there were times when I walked with her. One day I had a strange kind of flashback, and suddenly I felt like I was me again at her age, dragging my heels, carrying my bag, meandering along as I stumbled home from school. It was like all that water had never passed under the bridge and all that litter in the water had never gushed along.

Where did all that time go? How did I become this man who still feels like a little kid and yet he has a little kid of his own. How did it happen? I'm not a responsible adult. I haven't grown up. They should make you apply for a license to become a parent. For goodness sake you need one for a car or a puppy or a fishing spot!

One thing is certain – we dads have a big impact on the world. In my humble opinion anyway. So many people are influenced for good or bad by the behaviour of their old man. I’m grateful for the kindness and friendship of my dad who has always been such a gentleman. And now I'm an old man myself and somehow I have to find it in my wiring to shape up and not just be a big kid anymore.

I like the way God is portrayed as a good father – not just any old dad – but a caring, interactive, patient, interested, good parent. The literary selfies we find in Psalm 68 verse 5, Psalm 103 verses 13 and 14, and then in Luke's blog chapter 11 verses 11 to 13, portray a God who is the best kind of parent. One who understands that 'we are dust' – frail, flawed, going to get it wrong. That's what I need, not only a God who cares, but a God who understands. When I'm here behaving like a brat again, when I don't want to be a responsible adult, when I'm struggling to be a good parent myself. I need a God who has been there, a God who has walked amongst us misguided humans. Who knows the stuff of life, the kind of renegades we are.

The Greeks thought the gods were like children, not parents; spoilt, reactive, whiny and vindictive brats. Perhaps that was their way of making sense of life's chaos and unpredictability. They imagined heaven full of tantrum-hurlers, rattles flying out of cots all over the place. Hmm, trust me, you don't wanna God who's like a three year old. The Bible tells us that God's ways are not ours, his thoughts are different, his ways are his own. Have a look at Isaiah 55 verse 9. That's why we cannot fathom them, it would be like asking a three year old to fill in a tax return. Or a rubber duck to download an app.

We may make huge strides in understanding and ability, but we'll always be children when compared with the nature of God. Which can be problematic, because the more we perceive ourselves to be progressing, the less we like the idea that we are small. Not insignificant though. Never insignificant to a God who made the universe and yet crowned us humans with glory and honour. We have that on good authority from the writer of Psalm 8.

Echoes and Shadows

I feel like I spend half of my life trying to be happy and the other half trying to work out why I'm not.

I was chatting with a friend the other day about inter-planetary travel, (there is a link here, believe me) and how maybe we'll be able to do it in the afterlife. Wherever and whatever that is. Perhaps, in the future kingdom, the whole universe will be accessible and explorable.

In fact, there may well be entire planets dedicated to

Time travel
Mountain climbing
Deep sea diving
Winning
Creating
Communicating
Achieving greatness
Being a superhero
Ice cream consumption
Inter-galactic scrabble
Facebook – oh no sorry there already is a planet dedicated to that – earth
England winning every international sporting event (even football)
Not losing things (like car keys, glasses and TV remotes)

These longings we have, these wanderlusts, may well be echoes and shadows of desires from another world.
A place where all these things could be possible.
Maybe heaven is not just another world, but another world of worlds.

A universe of possibility where whole planets are given over to beaches and jungles and theme parks and libraries and graffiti walls and drive-in movies and art galleries and skateboard parks and roller-discos and late night parties.

That might explain why we crave them and chase them and plan them in this life. We're hungry for the possibilities of the next. However, the next world will certainly be a place where some things are *not* available. The sad endings, the goodbyes, the little deaths. And the big deaths too. No more tears, says John in his big screen Revelation, chapter 21.

When I first wrote this chapter my life was in a kind of turmoil. We were moving house, job, lifestyle… everything really. The world was shifting on its axis. Nothing was solid anymore. The ozone above me was melting and there was too much heat coming through. But there were good things about that as well as disturbing ones – a fresh start, new possibilities, the shedding of the old responsibilities.

There's a guy in the Good Book, Abraham, and one day he gets the clear notion that he should leave his father's house and move out into the unknown. Apparently the words 'father's house' for Abraham sum up everything he knows, everything that is safe and familiar to him. That's the kind of turmoil I sometimes feel we're facing as we move on. Leaving behind all that we have built around us. The walls tumble once again like pensioners blown around in the wind. And I wish for something solid. Something familiar. My father's house. But I have to move on. I have to let the boundaries crash.

Ultimately I guess I long for the safe clear view of the future life. That world of peace and exhilaration.

But the desert beckons, the distant voices of an earthly next life are calling, as we continue moving into the unknown. Which sounds poetic but when it's happening is jolly messy, it means half-packed boxes and jobs unfinished and a million address changes to sort out. Not romantic, heroic or poetic at all. Just a bit of a mountain to climb, and one with no flags or medals or records accompanying the journey.

The faint footprints of Abraham mark a shadowy path, I guess, and Christendom is littered with shabby saints who hit the highway in search of God's next place. Nomads and pilgrims in this life. We do our best to place one foot in front of the other, though, if you're anything like me, you long to settle and be safe.

Jesus Wouldn't Bother with Sermons

My daughter continues to watch *Horrible Histories* (again and again and again) and as a result is not only hugely entertained, but is learning stuff in the process. And so am I. Historyies Horriblis is a brilliant piece of TV, drawing on the rich cavern of our past lives and turning it into gruesome, enlightening entertainment. Literally car crash TV. You can't help but stop and gawp whenever you're passing through our lounge.

I read a challenging quote a while back in Derek Wilson's great book *The People's Bible* – all about the King James Bible, and the story of those who brought the Good Book to the people. Derek says, 'the church must continue to change, not with the world, but for the world.' He commented too on the danger of revering the King James Bible for its language alone, when it was written primarily to communicate with the general public. Maybe the best way to celebrate 400 plus years of bringing the Bible to the people is to continue to do just that. Continue to make it accessible to the public.

And that's where *Horrible Histories* comes in.

Entertainment is powerful. Jesus knew that. The old prophets knew it too. We can be sure of this because they were hugely entertaining. The pearls they brought to the people were not just hurled out there for the swine to trample, they were delivered in stories, jokes, sketches and anecdotes. Like *Horrible Histories*. Jesus drew on the media of his day and I am sure that today, in an age of huge media choice, Jesus would not be delivering sermons. That's my view anyway.

Which brings us, well me anyway, to the likes of *Inception*.

Inception is an incredibly inventive movie. I won't do it an injustice by trying to sum up in a couple of lines the wealth of ideas kicking about in its complex and entertaining storyline. It keeps you hooked while feeding your mind, stretching your soul and testing your perception. And I mention it because I'm sure there are ways to tell the Bible so that it keeps you hooked, feeds your mind, stretches your soul and tests your perception.

Like our own national horrible history, the Bible holds a shedload of fantastic stories, ripe for telling in gruesome, compelling and entertaining ways. But perhaps we must stop thinking of it as a book. It's a movie, a story, a joke told over a meal, a photograph, an advert, a viral video, a life lived, a page on Facebook, a blog, a Tweet, a sketch, a scribble, an hour of your life, a doodle, a facial expression, a job done well, a slap on the back, a kick up the ass... and so it goes on.

Let's think again and do an *Inception* and a *Horrible Histories* on it. Let's not just read it in our pulpits and churches and home groups and evangelistic meetings. Let's do something else with it, anything else. Let's just do it. Let's honour the memory and tireless work of those people who sweated, lived and died to bring the Bible to the people.

By bringing it to the people again.
Let's change. Not just with the world.

For the world.

The Brutal Bible

The *Horrible Histories* series has given me an idea. It made me wonder about a kind of *Brutal Bible*, a sort of *Gruesome Good Book* or an *Atrocious Apocrypha*, or perhaps the *Nifty New Testament*, or the *Odious Old One*. I think you get the point. So with that in mind, here's a quiz for you, a la Historiana Horriblis.

1. If you seduced a daughter of Jacob what was the punishment? Did you

a/ lose your eye?
b/ lose your marbles?
c/ lose a sensitive flap of skin off the end of your finger?
d/ lose a sensitive flap of skin off the end of your todger?

Answer... yes you guessed it – it's the todger one. Don't go expecting to get off with the hottie from Jake's house unless you're ready for not only you – but your whole town to get the end of their joysticks communally hacked... closely followed by all their other bits. Ouch! (Genesis chapter 34)

2. What sort of holiday should you not go on in the book of Judges?

a/ camping?
b/ wine making?
c/ lion wrestling?
d/ honey gorging?

Answer... well certainly not camping. You might get a tent peg through the skull, thanks to the lovely Jael (Judges chapter 4). Lion wrestling and honey gorging is fine if you've got long hair, an attitude problem and you're a spoilt brat called Samson (Judges chapter 14). Wine making is okay too, just don't get caught napping by an angel with Philistines on his mind (Judges chapters 6,7 & 8).

3. What was the best way to get heard in the Old Testament?

a/ do a striptease?
b/ become a mime artist?
c/ bury your knickers?
d/ set fire to your poo?

Answer... all of the above! Want to be a prophet? Then get ready to strip off, impersonate Mr Bean, stuff your boxers under the geraniums and burn your droppings. You have to feel sorry for Isaiah, Jeremiah, Micah and Ezekiel. Any wannabe prophets out there? It's a tough job and you need a pretty big drawer full of drawers.

How did you get on then?
3 out of 3 correct? You're clearly a Gruesome Good Book Genius.
2 out of 3? Definitely a Brutal Bible Boffin.
1 out of 3? An Odious Old Testament Expert.
0 out of 3? Try reciting aloud Job, Lamentations and Leviticus three times a day for the next six months.

Why? Why? Why? Delilah

Aggghhh!!!!!

Am I the only person in Christendom who can change a toilet roll? For goodness sake, I feel as if it must be a superpower or something. Apparently when it comes to replacing bottom-sprucing equipment I am Neo. Frodo. Harry. Paddington. I am *The One*. No one else in the known world has that power. Civilisation has been waiting for the Andrex messiah for centuries and I've finally got here. Sound like I'm ranting? You betcha. I'm weary of that sinking feeling you get when you see another brown cardboard tube with a few tatty strands of tissue paper hanging off it. And no way will a few tatty strands do the job.

And while I'm in rant central I might as well mention the movie *Hancock*. It isn't about that funny man Tony, but rather a chaotic dude with a superpower he didn't particularly want. When he has to rescue people (again!) he just tells them off for being idiots and getting into a jam in the first place. He has an anger problem, to go with his drinking and superpower problem. A dysfunctional superhero. Not unlike Little Big Man Samson, he who fell in love with the local hairdresser. Yea, Delilah, that's the one. If you have a Good Book around check out that bit they call Judges. Have a look at chapters 13 to 16. You won't find Kavanagh QC or Judge John or Rumpole of the Bailey knocking around in there, but you will find several unexpected heroes going by the names of Deborah, Jael, Gideon and Samson. Some of them have similarities with the hapless Hancock. Gideon was most reluctant at first (see Judges chapter 6 verse 15), and then, letting power go to his head, got very unpleasant (see Judges chapter 8 verses 57).

At times one or two biblical heroes look more like villains. For one thing they don't wear their pants over their tights, mainly because they don't wear tights. And, like Hancock, at times they blunder around, trying to make a difference and putting their foot in

a/ it
b/ their mouth,
c/ the camel dung, just before it hits the fan.

I take comfort from this. Because in my vain and pitiful attempts to follow Jesus, and make some kind of small difference in the world, I often put my foot in my mouth, just after placing it squarely in the dung. Sounds tasty eh?

The superheroes in the good book are more like Hancock than Superman. Hancock is reluctant, bad-tempered, and grouchy. So is Samson. Just look at the way he talks back to his parents.
Sam: Get me that Philistine woman!
Dad: Surely you could marry someone round here.
Sam: Oh that's soooooo unfair! I want her! Now! Get HER!!! You're so unfair!! GEEET HEEEEEEEERRRRRRR!!! Now! Now!! Now!!!

Gives us hope really.

Mind you, I doubt if Hancock could change a loo roll.

The Lion, The Witch and The Water Closet

I was musing on the idea of rewriting some of the classics, and I started by wondering about *The Lion, The Witch and The Sofa*, my daughter thought it would be great to fall down the back of the settee and land in snow.

But I was looking for another word beginning with W to replace Wardrobe. *The Lion, The Witch and The... Watermelon... Water-bottle...* (hot, obviously) *Whippet...*?

Eventually I ended up with *The Lion, The Witch and The Water Closet* – a sort of cross between the Aardman film *Flushed Away* and C.S. Lewis's *Narnia*. Fall down the toilet, flounder past some worrying-looking brown and green lumps, and fall flat on your face in a new land covered in off-white slush, populated by singing rats, bumbling pipe-playing fauns, talking badgers, dancing cockroaches and evil pest control people. Something like that. And obviously you need to put on a fur coat and play hide and seek before diving into the toilet in the first place. (Don't try this at home kids. Or adults.)

Anyway, this idea hasn't taken me very far yet, except that it made me wonder whether anyone might get upset at the analogy, turning C.S. Lewis's beloved classic into a dark malevolent faeces-strewn fantasy. As if Tim Burton had been one of the Inklings, replacing say... Mr Tolkein. (Actually on a J.R.R.T. note – how about *Lord of the Bins* – in which Frodo and his mates go on an adventure of epic proportions riding a council lorry, emptying people's dustbins, and sorting their recycling in an effort to find the one ring that will rule them all. This turns out to be a coffee-stain ring left on a discarded coaster, bearing the smiling face of Gollum, which needs to be hurled into Mount Doom, a massive pile of garbage somewhere near Milton Keynes. (Or perhaps it is Milton Keynes. ☺ No offence intended.)

But I digress. Messing with stories is one of the things I like about the Good Messiah. He was always taking stories that his mates knew and loved and giving them a twist to shock everybody, or make them laugh, or just plain annoy them. Certainly it made the tales powerful and memorable, because the folks who heard them repeated them again and again and again, eventually writing them down. One example, the tale of the rescuing Samaritan. If a story contained a Priest going home from the temple, closely followed by a Levite, then the next traveller would most certainly be a good Jewish layman. Obvious isn't it? Certainly it was to a first century Jewish audience. But wait a minute! What was that the carpenter just said? A Samaritan came along instead!! You're kidding right? No? But why?! What's that about? Let me just text that to my wife/husband.

So maybe next time you have an Armitage Shanks interface think on *The Lion, The Witch and The WC*, and the Good Messiah who took a tale about a good Jew who rescued his friend, and turned it into the Good Samaritan who rescued his enemy.

Happy flushing.

Emmaus Faith

D'you think he was wearing shades? Or maybe a false beard? Or a hoodie? Whichever way it seems to me that 'the incident of the God in the night-time' that was the Emmaus Road journey indicates one thing, Jesus has a cheeky sense of humour. He spends forever with these guys, pretending the whole time that he has no idea what's going on, and that he doesn't know anything about er... that Jesus of Nazareth guy. If you've got a Bible handy check it if you like in Luke's blog chapter 24 round about verse 13.

This is a very different Jesus to the pre-resurrection man. Before that death-defying resurrection moment (surely the greatest flash mob incident in history) it had been all about – watch me, learn from me, see how I treat people, take note, see how I operate, observe closely... then go and mimic me. Now things are a little different. On that road out of Jerusalem, with two disciples running away from the faith, at the key moment when he breaks bread, the shekel drops and they realise it's him – kerbam! – he disappears. He's gone. The post-resurrection Jesus is a kind of Catch-me-if-you-can figure. Now you see me, now you don't.

Jesus in disguise. The hidden God.

Ever feel that? As if you're following a shy Messiah? A shadowy, silhouetted figure. You have to look hard, concentrate, keep your eyes peeled, just in case you might miss that sudden – ping – 'here I am' moment.

It seems to me that the Emmaus Road story, as told in Luke's gospel blog, in the chapter we now call 24, was the start of something big. Something different. The beginning of faith as we know it today. Where's your God then? People might say. Show us and we might just believe. Well, he's there, no he's there. No, he's over there. And over here. He's in that wink, that tear, that joke, that scream, that smile. Etc. etc.

Everybody wants proof of course. We'd all prefer that. Ever since Adam swapped *life* for *knowledge* in that old garden called Eden; that old offer he couldn't refuse, from that old devil called Hissing Sid. It would be much easier to have a Jesus who is visibly present, wearing a wristband that said 'What Would I Do', but it seems he won't play that game. He wants us to own our faith, to do what those boys in *Dead Poets Society* did when they started copying the departing Mr Keating. They'd seen their poetry teacher stand on the desk, so hey, they thought 'we can do that too', and in tribute to their departing leader they got off their backsides and jumped on their desks. No more Mr Keating? Well, now there's a roomful of Mr Keating wannabes.

The Emmaus Road tale kicks off a time of getting on the desks. The Invisible Messiah is no longer around in the way he used to be when he laughed with prostitutes, wrestled with fishermen and hung out with the marginalised. Must be our turn then. He's coaxing this reluctant disciple to stand up, say, 'Captain my Captain' and practically join in with the things he did.

Just keep an eye open for that guy with the shades and the false beard and the hoodie pulled low. It could be him again, pulling alongside with a smile on his face, as he asks us, in the guise of a stranger, what's on our minds.

Somewhere Between Our Things and Our Stuff

One final reflection on the throes of moving house. You open cupboards and suddenly the house fills with so much stuff you can barely expand your chest to breathe out. Where does all this stuff come from? I quickly find myself depressed and weary from packing and shifting and unpacking and unshifting. It goes on and on and on. I'd throw it away or give it away but strangely I lack the emotional energy and backbone. I've never been good at simplifying.

The movie *Bobby* is about the night Bobby Kennedy got shot, and the people who were in the hotel where the shooting took place. One of the characters, Samantha, is insecure, like most of us, and rates herself according to what she owns and wears. Her husband Jack treats her the way Jesus treated so many of the folks he met, he sits her down and shows her what matters in her life. He slows here up for a moment, pulls back life's confusing curtain, and gives her a glimpse of reality. He says something along the lines of, 'You and I are more than those things we own. Somewhere between our things and our stuff is the real us.'

The good Messiah once said something about worry, and how the flowers and birds don't fret the way we do. (Memorably rehashed in a few lines from the film *Life of Brian* – Brian: 'Consider the birds…' One of the crowd: 'Oh leave the birds alone…' Brian: 'All right, consider the lilies…' One of the crowd: 'Oh he's having a go at the flowers now!')

Seems to me that Jesus understood what Jack can see in the film *Bobby*, that stuff can easily weigh us down, it strong-arms us into comparing ourselves with others and leaves a ravenous gash in our hearts so that we simply long for more.

A crevice too big to ever fill. A monster too hungry to satisfy. Years ago I heard a saying which went something like this: 'The creator made things to be used and people to be loved. And we can easily get it the wrong way round.'
‘Guard your heart,’ says the Good Book, ‘for from it flow the springs of life. Look after it, for it affects everything you do.’

I’ll finish with a little parable of my own.

The human heart is rather like an old attic. It's a place of storage, a place of memories. We wander through it and discover things long forgotten, things we kept for a rainy day, things we have hidden. We seldom take our visitors there and even our families only get a rare glimpse. But sometimes, on vacant rainy days we may drag the one we most love up those dusty steps through the cobwebs and memories and share an hour of laughter and hope, healing and tears as we uncover what we most treasure and most fear. The human heart is a place of storage, but like any attic, it may only hold so much, so we do well to fill it with precious things.

Thanks for reading.

Dave

Made in the USA
Columbia, SC
23 June 2017